AF541219

LITERACY CAMPAIGN IN INDIA

LITERACY CAMPAIGN IN INDIA

By

M.Soundarapandian

DISCOVERY PUBLISHING HOUSE
NEW DELHI-1100 02

Published by:

DISCOVERY PUBLISHING HOUSE PVT. LTD.
4383/4B, Ansari Road, Darya Ganj
New Delhi-110 002 (India)
Phone : +91-11-23279245; 23253475; 43596065
E-mail : discoverybooksindia@gmail.com
discoverypublishinghouse@gmail.com
namitwasan9@gmail.com
web : www.discoverypublishinggroup.com

First Published: **2000**
Reprinted: **2022**

ISBN: 978-81-7141-553-3

Literacy Campaign in India

© Author

All rights reserved. No part of this publication should be reproduced, stored in a retrieval system, or transmitted in any form or by any means: electronic, mechanical, photocopying, recording or otherwise, without the prior written permission of the author and the publisher.

This book has been published in good faith that the material provided by authors is original. Every effort is made to ensure accuracy of material, but the publisher and printer will not be held responsible for any inadvertent error(s). In case of any dispute, all legal matters are to be settled under Delhi jurisdiction only.

Printed at:
Infinity Imaging Systems
Delhi

PREFACE

Literacy is the stepping stone towards the solution of many crucial problems. A man without literacy is blind, handicapped, crippled throughout his life. Hence, it is rightly said, "Education (Literacy) is the second birth (Dwitiya Janma). Man may not get salvation without Education (Literacy). Literacy promotes human resource which is very important for the nation. Literacy is the Key to progress.

In India, in the beginning of the present century (1901) the literacy rate was just 5.3 percent. After independence (1951) literacy rate increased to 16.7 percent. Indian constitution made a provision to provide free and compulsory primary education upto the age of 14 through article 45 with a view to promote literacy. But we failed to achieve this target. Functional education was started during the year 1967-68. In 1975, Non-formal Education programme for the age group 15-25 was introduced.

During the decade 1982-91 significant steps were taken by the government towards promotion of literacy. The National Policy on Education (NPE) was approved by the parliament in 1986 and its programme of action was approved in the same year. The year 1987 was the year of launching new schemes. In 1988, National Literacy Mission (NLM) was established for imparting functional literacy to 80 million illiterate persons. Apart from imparting functional literacy, the Mission aims at conscientising the learners to some values like national integration, conservation of the environment, women's equality and family planning.

Under the auspices of NLM. Total Literacy Campaigns (TLC), Post Literacy Campaigns (PLC) and Continuing Education Programme (CEP) are being implemented in several districts of the country.

The objective of the Book is to analyse the performance of the Literacy Campaigns in eradicating illiteracy and empowering the beneficiaries of the programme. As a key Resource Person of Kamarajar District Literacy Campaign, I have visited many centres of the literacy campaigns. The State Resource Centre for Non-Formal Education, Chennai and Bharat Gyan Vigyan Samiti, New Delhi had provided assistance for conducting the evaluation studies in various districts of Tamil Nadu on many themes like Dropouts, Enrollment, Needs and Interests on Reading Material, Entrepreneurship Development etc. The analytical evaluation of various studies and practical experience gave a birth to this book of 'Literacy Campaign in India'. The book highlights the concept, experience, successful achievements and difficulties in the implementation of the Literacy Campaign in Tamil Nadu.

I am thankful to the State Resource Centre for Non-formal Education, Chennai and Bharat Gyan Vigyan Samiti, New Delhi for their assistance in conducting the field survey. I extended my thanks to Dr. R. Rajan, State Resource Centre for Non–formal Education for his encouragement in completing the project works. I am indebted to Dr. N. Thillainayagam, professor and Head, Department of Rural Industries and Management, Gandhigram for his inspiring advice in completing this endeavour. The untiring support extended by my wife Mrs. S. Indhymathy and my children Diwarkaran and Vidya, helped me to enjoy the completion of this work. Finally, my sincere thanks to the Discovery Publishing House for their acceptance in publishing the book.

M. Soundarapandian
Gandhigram.

CONTENTS

1. Total Literacy Campaign: A Review 1

2. Drop-outs in Total Literacy Campaign 30

3. Total Literacy Campaign on School Enrolment and Dropouts 58

4. Reading Materials to the Neo - Literates Under Post Literacy Campaign 79

5. Population Education Message to Neo Literates 116

6. Literacy Campaign and Empowerment 160

Bibliography 177

Index 185

1

TOTAL LITERACY CAMPAIGN: A REVIEW

INTRODUCTION

Illiteracy as a mass phenomenon blocks economic and social progress, affects adversely economic productivity, population control, national integration and improvement in health and sanitation. Illiterate people fail to appreciate national efforts directed to raising the standard of people and are generally immunised to the national call for working whole heartedly towards fulfillment of running democratic form of Government smoothly. We have chosen to be a democracy and adopt socialistic pattern of society, the success of which would largely depend upon enlightened masses. Undoubtedly, illiteracy is a serious impediment to one's own growth as also to socio-economic progress and to the political stability of the country.

Elimination of illiteracy has been one of the major concerns of our Government since independence. With more than four decades of freedom it has not been possible to eliminate illiteracy which in turn is the underlying cause of other problems faced by the country such as object poverty, unemployment, population growth, unhygienic conditions, exploitation and superstitions. It is really surprising that the country is going to have world's largest number of illiterates by the turn of the century.

According to recent World Bank study if the speed of eradicating illiteracy is not accelerated, the country will account for more than half of illiterate population of world. It is not being realised that because of illiteracy and ignorances vast majority of our people have not been able to take advantage of massive investment.

The Government has made through various development programmes and schemes to raise the standard of living in this country. Consequently a large segment of our population is still below the poverty line. It is, therefore, rightly asserted by the Director General of UNESCO that education is a key to the future and literacy is the most essential of all educational skills. Research all over the world has also proved that literacy drive is a powerful instrument of economic development and social change in a country.

Adult Education Programme has not achieved the desired results because of the many hurdles such as lack of commitment on the part of implementing agencies, lack of missionary zeal, inadequate school support, non-involvement of voluntary agencies and the fatalistic attitude of illiterates.

It has been estimated that if past trends continue, and no significant acceleration occurs in the rate of expansion of literacy, India could well end up with the dubious distinction of being home to more than half the world's non-literates by 2000 A.D. To prevent such a denouement, it is important to undertake, on a war footing, a massive national effort aimed simultaneously at eradication of illiteracy and universalistion of primary education.

The National Literacy Mission (NLM) was established in 1988, with the objective of revising and strengthening the existing adult education programmes in the country and to imparting functional literacy to 80 million illiterate persons in the 15-35 age group by 1995. To be 'literate' in terms of the norms of the NLM, a learner must have basic literacy and numerary skills, functional knowledge usable in day-to-day affairs and social awareness. The focus of the Mission is on rural areas and particularly on women and persons belonging to the scheduled castes and scheduled tribes. Apart from imparting functional literacy, the mission aims at consientising the learners to values of national integration, conservation of the environment, women's equality, family planning, etc., and making them aware of the causes of their deprivation to enable them to move towards the amelioration of their condition through organisation and participation in the process of development.

The Total Literacy Campaign Model was developed for achieving mass literacy from the experience of the campaign implemented by the Kerala Shastra Sahitya Parished (KSSP) in Ernakulam District. Under the auspices of NLM, the TLCs are implemented in more than 200 districts through the Bharat Gyan Vigyan Samiti (BGVS). Several districts in the country had achieved 'fully literate' status by December 1992. A few of them are Burdwan and Mindnapur in West Bengal, the entire Union Territory of Pondicherry, Narsinghpur in Madhya Pradesh, Nizamabad in Andhra Pradesh, Sundergrah in Orissa, Bijapur in Karnataka and Pasumpon. Pudukottai and Kamarajar Districts in Tamil Nadu.

A study has been conducted to review the experiences of TLCs in the successful implementation in various states of our country and in some other countries. Secondary data were collected from the reports of NLM, office records of TLC, books, journals and newspapers for the study. The primary data for analysing the problems of implementation of TLC were collected by field visits in 20 campaign centres in Kamarajar District of Tamil Nadu and by interviewing the learners, volunteer instructors other implementors.

LITERACY STATUS IN INDIA:

An unpleasant global picture of illiteracy is noticed with the following realities.

(i) More than 100 million children including 60 million girls have no access at all to primary schooling.

(ii) More than 960 million adults, two-third of whom are women, are illiterate. Functional illiteracy is a significant problem in all countries.

(iii) More than one-third of the world's adults have no access to printed knowledge, new skills and technologies that could improve the quality of their lives.

(iv) More than 100 million children and countless adults fail to complete basic education programmes.

The world conference on "Education for All" held in Jomtien, Thailand in 1990 adopted a Declaration which proclaimed "Every person-child, youth and adult shall be able to benefit from educational opportunities designed to meet their basic learning need. Their needs comprise both essential learning tools (such as literacy, oral expression, numerary and problem solving) and the basic learning content (such as knowledge, skills, values and attitudes) required by human beings to be able to survive, to develop their full capacities, to live and work within dignity of their lives, to make informed decisions, and to continue learning". After six years of Jomtien Declaration, we are not even nearer to the goal achieving education for children by 2000.

Nine most populous countries of the World - China, India, Bangladesh, Brazil, Indonesia, Egypt, Nigeria, Mexico and Pakistan - participated in the New Delhi Summit on "Education for All" held in December 1993. According to UNESCO estimates these nine countries have (1) seventy percent of the World's population (2) half of World's out of school children, and (3) two-thirds of World's illiterates. Seventy million in these countries are still outside the ambit of primary education. India accounts for one-third of the World's unlettered and twenty percent of out of-school children. The summit held in Delhi was not only timely but also the resolutions of the summit were of great importance for making education available to all.

There were 948 million adult non-literates in the world in 1990 of whom 65 percent were female. Ten countries accounted for 705 million non-literates. India and China accounted for more than half the non-literates. Female illiteracy was particularly striking in Asia which accounted for 77 percent of the female non-literates. A disturbing fact to note is that, of the increase in non-literate from 1960 to 1985, 86 percent were women.

Within this general pattern, let us look at India's literacy status in relation to co-operable countries. Table-1 provides data on literacy rates and primary school enrolment ratios for 14 developing countries each of which has a population exceeding 50 million. Except for Turkey, which is a European outliner in the sample, the countries account for practically all the 'large' developing countries in Asia, Africa and Latin America.

TABLE 1

Adult Literacy and Primary Education - Select Inter-country Comparisons

Sl. No.	Name of the Country	Adult Literacy percent 1990		Primary School Enrolment, percentage of Age group			
				1965		1989	
		Total	Female	Total	Female	Total	Female
1.	Bangladesh	35	22	49	31	70	64
2.	Brazil	81	80	108	105	108	-
3.	China	73	62	89	-	135	128
4.	Egypt	48	34	75	60	97	89
5.	India	48	34	74	57	98	82
6.	Indonesia	77	68	72	65	118	115
7.	Iran	54	43	63	40	109	101
8.	Mexico	87	85	92	90	114	112
9.	Nigeria	51	39	32	24	70	63
10.	Pakistan	35	21	40	20	38	27
11.	Philippines	90	89	113	111	114	110
12.	Thailand	93	90	78	74	-	-
13.	Turkey	81	71	101	83	112	108
14.	Vietnam	88	84	-	-	-	-

Source: World Development Report, 1992 World Bank, Washington, D.C.

The data on primary school enrolment rates show a family close correspondence with literacy rates. India fares marginally better with regard to primary school enrollment ratios, ahead of Nigeria and Thailand besides Pakistan and Bangladesh, but even here the progress between 1965 and 1989 is modest. Iran has overtaken India in this period while china has forged rapidly ached. Nigeria, way behind in 1965, has closed a good part of the gap between then and 1989.

The simple, unambiguous message from the data presented in Table-1 is that unless India makes a massive effort, both mounting a direct, large scale attack on adult illiteracy, and ensuring rapid universalisation of primary education, it will remain near the bottom of the world literacy league.

The ratio of literates to population is useful indicator. However, for policy purposes and in line with international norms, it is fruitful to look at the literacy status of the population aged 7 years and above. Table-2 presents the data on ratio of literates to population in the age group of 7 years and above.

It is evident that progress in literacy since Independence has not been of uniform pace. The rapid improvement in literacy recorded between 1951 and 1961 was not sustained through the two decades 1961-81. The percentage point increase between 1981 and 1991 is some what more encouraging, especially in repeat of the female literacy rates.

TABLE 2:

All India Literacy Rates (percent) by sex, population Aged 7 years and above, 1951-91.

Year	Total	Male	Female
1951	19.74	29.00	12.87
1961	30.11	42.96	16.32
1971	36.49	48.92	23.00
1981	43.56	56.37	29.75
1991	52.11	63.86	39.42

Source: Prem Chand, Literacy Digest, Directorate of Adult Education, Government of India, New Delhi.

Table 2 presents data for 1981 and 1991 on ratios of literates to population for each major State, separately for total, rural and urban populations. Since we are essentially looking at rural-urban differences, the fact that 1991 data pertains to literates aged 7 years and above while the data for 1981 relate to literates aged 5 years and above can be ignored for purposes of comparison.

The data are really striking. They show that both in 1981 and in 1991, with the sole exception of Kerala, urban literacy ratios exceed rural ones considerably. In 1981 except of Kerala, the percentage points difference exceeds 20 in all cases. In 1991, the picture is pretty much the same, except that apart from Kerala, Punjap also shows a less than 20 percentage points difference between urban and rural literacy ratios, though it is still quite large at 17.63 percentage points.

What is also noteworthy is the fact that even states like Tamil Nadu, Maharastra and Gujarat which report literacy ratios significantly above the national average exhibit large urban-rural differences is both 1991 and 1981. Typically, the low literacy states also show a larger urban-rural literacy gap. Thus Bihar, Madhya Pradesh and Rajasthan show the biggest urban-rural differences.

The data demonstrate that the urban-rural gap has narrowed only marginally between 1981 and 1991 in most cases. In the case of Bihar and Orissa, the gap has actually increased, though again only marginally.

Details apart, the data bring out clearly the extremely dismal literacy situation in practically all of rural India, with the sole exception of Kerala, where the gap between urban and rural literacy rate had come down to just 4.25 percentage points in 1991. By contrast, in Bihar, Madhya Pradesh and Rajasthan, the Urban literacy ratio was more than twice the rural ratio.

It needs to be emphasised that one cannot look at the target population of adult non-literate-be it 150,180 or 200 million in static terms. Every year, primary school dropouts are being added to the pool of non-literates. It should also be noted that the primary school dropout non-enrolment phenomenon is especially actuate in the populous, low literacy states. Table 4 presents data on gross enrolment ratios in classes I to V, percentage of girls' enrolment to total enrolment in primary school, and enrolment in class V as percentage of enrolment in class I as of 1986. The low literacy states of Bihar, Madhya Pradesh, Rajasthan and Uttar Pradesh all report low ratios of girls' enrolment to total enrolment: as low as 28 percent in the case of Rajasthan, just around one third in the case of Bihar and Uttar Pradesh, and around three-eighths in the case of Madhya Pradesh.

With the some what surprising exception of Madhya Pradesh and Uttar Pradesh, the low literacy status of Andra Pradesh, Orissa, Rajasthan and Bihar also report high drop-out rates. In the country as a whole, only Kerala reports a near -zero dropout rate as well as nearly equal enrolment of boys and girls in primary school. Even states like Maharastra and Tamil Nadu with high enrolment ratios have rather high dropout rates.

All of this suggest that a considerable non-literates in the form of non-enrolled and drop-out children are being added to the already

TABLE 1.3 :
Ratio of Literates to Population, Total Rural and Urban, Major States, 1981 and 1991.

Sl. No.	State	1981 Total %	1981 Rural %	1981 Urban %	1981 Rural Urban Difference % points	1991 Total %	1991 Rural %	1991 Urban %	1991 Urban Rural Difference % points
1.	Andhra Pradesh	29.94	23.24	51.99	28.75	37.58	30.55	56.82	26.27
2.	Assam	-	-	-	-	43.20	39.94	69.95	30.01
3.	Bihar	26.20	22.50	52.18	29.68	31.11	27.18	59.99	29.81
4.	Gujarat	43.70	36.20	60.31	24.11	51.69	44.80	64.83	20.03
5.	Harayana	36.14	30.33	56.86	26.53	45.53	40.26	61.48	21.22
6.	Karnataka	38.46	31.05	56.71	25.66	47.27	39.63	64.33	24.70
7.	Kerala	70.42	69.11	76.11	7.00	78.09	76.97	81.22	4.25
8.	Madhya pradesh	27.87	21.22	54.02	32.80	35.51	28.48	58.79	30.31
9.	Maharastra	47.18	38.15	63.92	25.77	54.53	45.95	68.10	22.15
10.	Orissa	34.23	31.49	54.77	23.28	40.97	37.76	61.70	23.94
11.	Punjab	40.86	35.21	55.63	20.42	49.28	44.04	61.67	17.63
12.	Rajasthan	24.38	17.99	48.35	30.36	31.04	24.20	54.08	29.88
13.	Tamil Nadu	46.76	38.56	63.45	24.89	56.62	47.60	67.99	20.39
14.	Uttar pradesh	27.16	23.06	45.88	22.82	33.84	29.70	50.52	20.82
15.	West Bengal	40.94	33.12	62.66	29.54	48.13	41.21	66.49	25.28
16.	India	36.23	29.65	57.40	27.75	42.89	36.36	61.78	25.42

Source: 1. R.S. Mathur, et.al, Literacy Digest, Directorate of Adult Education, Government of India, New Delhi, 1988.
2. Prem chand, Literacy Digest, Directorate of Adult Education, Government of India, New Delhi, 1991.

massive pool of non-literates. It has been estimated that if past trends continue, and no significant acceleration occurs in the rate of expansion of literacy, India could well end up with the dubious distinction of being home to more than half the World's non-literates by 2000 AD. To prevent such a denouement, it is important to undertake, on a war footing, a massive national effort aimed simultaneously at eradication of illiteracy and universalisation of primary education.

TABLE 4
Some Indicators of Primary Education

Sl. No.	State	Boys	Girls	Total	Percentage of Girls Enrolment in total Enrolment	Enrolment in class as % of that in class I
1.	Andhra pradesh	128.39	117.83	123.18	47.24	38.02
2.	Assam	98.40	81.21	90.09	43.52	37.09
3.	Bihar	105.20	52.77	79.13	33.16	34.47
4.	Gujarat	119.84	95.31	107.86	43.18	50.61
5.	Harayana	95.81	77.60	87.35	41.28	68.52
6.	Karnataka	117.70	98.69	108.33	44.90	47.50
7.	Kerala	106.71	104.59	105.67	48.79	98.84
8.	Madhya Pradesh	116.31	76.33	96.86	38.35	64.14
9	Maharastra	125.82	107.21	116.69	45.05	54.67
10.	Orissa	110.36	81.87	96.24	42.10	47.10
11.	Punjab	97.03	92.85	95.08	45.58	65.15
12.	Rajasthan	104.08	50.62	80.31	28.02	27.55
13.	Tamil Nadu	125.77	120.01	123.06	45.97	67.79
14.	Uttar Pradesh	86.17	50.33	69.29	34.21	58.57
15.	West Bengal	87.16	70.17	78.86	43.44	38.15
16.	India	106.42	79.89	93.63	41.16	49.28

Source: Fifth All India Educational Survey) National Council of Educationl Research and Training, New Delhi, 1989), Table 27,28, and 29 p.p.66-71.

LITERACY MOVEMENT IN INDIA

Literacy work for common men and women was started in India during the last quarter of the 19th century by social reformers. As a result literacy classes were conducted and libraries, reading rooms were opened. But these were confined to only a few pockets in the country where social reformers could muster enough strength to organise such activities.

During the British rule it was Lord Macanlay who established schools to promote literacy. In the beginning of the present century (1901) the literacy rate was just 5.3 percent. It means out of 100 people only five were literate.

In 1920, under the leadership of Mahatma Gandhi, the struggle for freedom took the form of "Mass Movement", which released abundant energy throughout the country. After the suspension of the movement in 1922 Gandhi directedthis stupendous energy towards constructive programme like organisation of night schools and literacy classes. Classes were conducted in cities, towns and villages for illiterate adults.

National schools and colleges which owed their existence to the mass movement, took active part in literacy work. A few provincial governments also made provision in their budgets for adult literacy. People with political awareness, their leaders and a few provincial governments continued to pay attention to literacy work. But it could not gain momentum.

The literacy work took the shape of a mass movement in 1937 after the installation of Congress Ministries in the province. The first Mass Literacy drive was launched in Bihar by setting up of a Mass Literacy Committee through area committees entursted teachers, students and others to organise literacy classes on voluntary basis.

The literacy work in the field was supplemented by literature published for the purpose and by the establishment of village libraries. More than 6 percent increase in the literacy figures during the decade 1931-41 however, seems to a great extent due to the mass literacy movement. But after the resignation of the Congress Government in 1939, the movement came to an abrupt end. Most of the libraries set up during the mass movement quickly went out of existence.

After the mass literacy movement was suspended, literacy work was continued to Bombay and Mysore by non-official organisation with financial assistance from the state Governments, cultural and social programmes, reading clubs and libraries.

Some of the agencies developed the use of wall newspapers as a medium for general education. Others organised residential education programmes for general education and for creating general awareness. Some others directed their devotion towards women's education. They developed programmes and activities around diversified things such as child care, family welfare, health education, sewing, embroidery, knitting and doll making.

After independence (1951) literacy rate increased to 16.7 percent. Indian constitution made a provision to provide free and compulsory primary education up to the age of 14 through Article 45 with a view to promote literacy. Gradually after independence, literacy got last into a maze of multifarious programmes and activities started under social education. Social education took the place of 'Adult Education', creating general awareness and civic consciousness among the people.

It was only in 1959, that the idea of mass movement for literacy was experimented in Maharastra. But the rate of growth was very slow and so the planners realised the urgency of taking effective steps to tackle the problem of illiteracy. An experimental project known as "Worker's Social Education Institute" was started by the Ministry of education at the end of the first five year plan.

Towards the end of the Third Five Year Plan, the planning commission approved the idea of state Governments initiating pilot projects in the field of literacy. Though some State Governments started organising literacy campaigns, they had not institutional base and lacked continuity. There was either none or inadequate follow-up programme. The result was considerable wastage of efforts and revenue.

During the fourth plan period, the work of spreading literacy among the masses was left to voluntary concentrated on conducting the Farmer's Functional Literacy Programme (1967-68). It was a part of the experimental world Literacy Programme and was confined to the districts chosen for introducing high yielding varieties of seeds and a package of improved agricultural practices.

Another scheme of Urban Adult Education was started by the Ministry of Education with the assistance of UNESCO in 1967 for establishing polyvalent Adult Education centres to organise integrate educational and training courses. The work of these experiments was found satisfactory and it was considered worthwhile to continue these efforts and improve and extend them further.

Functional education was started during the year 1967-68. In 1975 non-formal education programme for the age group 15-25 was introduced. In 1978 National Adult Education programme (NAEP) was introduced for the age group 15-35. The outline of NAEP for eradication of illiteracy was discussed at the first meeting of the National Board of Adult Education established in 1977, on the recommendation of the Kothari Commission. The programme was, however, formally inaugurated on 2nd October 1978. The target on NAEP was to cover by 1984, the entire illiterate population in the 15-35 age group. The success of NAEP as a mass movement will be determined by the extent to which youth and students can be motivated to commit themselves to this programme.

In 1981, the census report reveals that the literacy rate was raised to 36 percent. During the decade 1982-1991 significant steps were taken by the government towards promotion of literacy. The Government has accorded high priority to adult education programmes by including it under the Minimum Needs programme in the Sixth Five year plan and under the New Twenty point programme. The Government of India provides grants in aid to voluntary organisations working in the field of adult education.

The National Policy of Education (NEP) was approved by the parliament in 1986 and its Programme of Action was also approved in the same year. The year 1987 was the year of launching new schemes. The 1981 census showed that male literacy in India was about 47 percent while female literacy was 25 percent. Thus the female literacy was much lower. The NPE envisages that education will be used as an agent of basic change in the status of women.

Programmes of the late 1970s and the 1980s have had neither a mass character nor the quality associated with selective intensive projects. While the project approach of these programmes stressed that a project should be in a compact and contiguous area, they neither required total coverage in the project area nor prevented the scattering of project sites. As a result, and in the context of the magnitude of the problem of illiteracy, the NAEP was supposed to tackle, its intensity and spread remained rather limited.

A new Programme of Action (POA) was prepared in line with the New Education Policy 1986. The POA announces a new National Programme of Adult education (NAPAE) which was to be a phased time-bound programme, covering approximately 40 million by 1990 and another 60 million by 1995.

NPAE was essentially a continuation of the then on going schemes of Rural Functional Literacy Projects (RFLP), State Adult Education programmes (SAEP) and the programme of assistance to voluntary agencies. In addition to these programmes, the Mass programme of Functional Literacy (MPFL) envisaged students education institutions, trade unions, local bodies and other individual organisations taking up literacy work voluntarily on an 'each one-teach one' basis, with provisions of reimbursement for actual field expenses incurred by them. This component was intended to give a market slant to the N' AE from the present intensive selective activity on a limited scale to a mass Programme.

The NPAE document put forward the idea of a technology mission for the eradication of illiteracy. in pursuance of this commitment, the National Literacy Mission (NLM) was launched on 5 May 1988. It has also been noted that while the NLM is partly a by-product of the National policy on Education-1986, it was largely the outcome of an evaluation of the strengths and weaknesses of the NAEP by the Institutes of Social Research and Management.

In quantitative terms, the key objective of the Mission was to impart functional literacy to 80 million persons in the 15-35 age group in two phases: 30 million by 1990 and an additional 50 million by 1995. Motivation was identified as the central issue in literacy, and the design of the mission was to be based on this understanding. The Mission document also spoke of efforts to secure people's participation, involve voluntary agencies, improve on going programmes like the KFLP and the SAEP, expand the mass programme of functional literacy and institutionalize post literacy and continuing education.

The national level management structure for the NLM provides for a autonomous body in the Department of Education of the Union Ministry of Human Resource Development called the National Literacy Mission Authority (NLMA). Vested with extensive financial and executive powers, the NLMA has a two tier structure: (i) The council, headed by the Union Minister for Human Resource Development and including/among others, ministers, leaders of major political parties, Members of parliament and educationalists (ii) The executive Committee (EC) headed by the Union Education Secretary. The Executive Committee of the NLMA would meet regularly and serve as the operational leadership of the Mission within the broad parameters of policy enunciated by the council.

Within a few months of the launching of the NLM, two new development took place which were to transform totally the character and future course of development of the NLM, and of the literacy scenario and outlook in the country. These dramatic development came in the form of two initiatives: one proposed and implemented by the Kerala Sastra Sahitya Parished, the most experienced and leading contingent of India's growing "People's Movement" and the other by the `Bharat Gyan Vigyan Samiti".

TLC - A NEW CONCEPT

In India, centre-based approaches for adult and non-formal education for several decades failed to achieve any real progress in the field of mass literacy. The success of the new TLC model depends mainly on the distinguishing features of the campaign. The three innovative features of the TLC are : Mass Campaign Approach, Participatory Approach and Voluntary Approach.

i) **Mass Campaign Approach:** Typically a TLC has as its territory a compact geographical-administrative area, usually a district. It seeks to cover a specific target of illiterate population in a specified age group of 15-35 years. It is also time-bound. usually a year.

ii) **Participatory Approach** : The people at all levels are encouraged to participate actively in the campaign by joining literacy committees at the district, block, panchayat or village levels, literacy street-theater groups, academic committees and so on.

iii) **Voluntary Approach:** The entire work of imparting literacy to learners is done on a voluntary basis. Some full time project staff are working far beyond the normal hours of work and earn a minimum amount of honorarium.

In the TLC approach, there is an inbuild system of motivation for the learners and volunteer instructors. For example. a high-pitched environment building drive is undertaken right from the beginning, involving all sections of the community and especially women, students, teachers and others. This exercise lasts for nearly two to three months prior to the start of the actual teaching-learning process. There is door-to-door canvassing at the time of survey to identify potential learners in the different areas.

The factors such as cost-effectiveness, decentralised and non-bureaucratic character, mass participation, time-bound nature and significant multidimensional societal impact make the TLC model attractive. Because of these and other reasons an attempt is made in the TLC districts to impart functional literacy to the learners which can help in empowering the deprived sections of the community and lead to social change.

The other main features are:

a. **Creation of a suitable environment for learning**: By means of massive publicity campaign making use of posters, banners, stickers, notices and the mass media but largely focussed in local art forms in the 'Kala Jatha' or similar style.
b. **Maximal community participation and involvement:** It must become a 'People's Movement'.
c. **Massive mobilization of volunteers:** On an average, for every 10 illiterates there must be one volunteer instructor. In addition, one needs volunteers for cultural programmes, padayatras, organization work and so on.
d. **Training**: A massive and specially designed training programme conducted in camps, involving thousands of master trainers and

instructors. Through these camps' motivation, awareness and pedagogic skills are imparted to the volunteers.

e. **Single Organisational structure**: The coming together of all forces - governmental and non- government - including senior officials, elected representatives, both legislative and panchayat, voluntary organisation, trade union activities, social workers etc., into a single organizational command structure. Such a pooling of all available resources is mandatory for literacy.

f. **Size of the project**: The optimal size of the project is taken as a district. The district, with the collector as its head, is a well manageable administrative unit where in the collector has considerable powers.

g. **Suitability**: The timings, venue etc., are decided between the volunteers and learners with the village committee's guidance.

h. **Flexilbility :** A flexible 5-6 months duration syllabus under the I P C L guidelines. These are adopted to the needs of the district. The course is usually divided into 3 primers each covering literacy and numerary lessons and inbuilt evaluation tests.

i. **Management and Information System**: An efficient well viable management and information structure or monitoring and evaluation structure which regularly keeps track of the functioning, assesses levels of learning, which can initiate corrective steps wherever needed.

j. **Time Bound**: Finally, the entire programme is time bound, usually a 3 months campaign followed by simultaneous start of teaching that lasts for 5-6 months and a consolidation phase that takes a variable period. In practice learning centres do not start in all areas and some persons and centres start as late as 6 months after the first set, making extension of time necessary.

MASS LITERACY CAMPAIGN IN OTHER COUNTRIES

Mass Literacy Campaign have typically been born of ideological commitment, on the one hand, and utilitarian consideration of nation building and socio-economic development on the other. For literacy campaigns, there must be matching of ideas among politicians, development planners, and literacy educators. This can be promoted by bringing them together at national level symposia. The role of the intelligent in each country is significant in preparing the ground for the campaign.

There have been a number of successful Mass Literacy Campaigns all over the world. They have taken place under a variety of political and historical conditions, ranging from Sweden in mid sixteenth century to Nicaragua in the 1980s. While each National Mass Literacy Campaign has no doubt its own unique features, certain generalisations also emerge from a study of these campaigns.

The National Adult Literacy Campaign of the USSR came officially into being with the signature by V.L. Lenine on 26 December 1919. It was in 1939 that the Literacy Campaign was officially closed. However, it was not lack of will, faulty direction or insufficient efforts under which the Literacy Campaign was declared. The encompassed all fifteen republics and the whole population between 8 and 50 years old.

The Vietnamese Mass Literacy Campaign was launched during October 1945 and December 1946. I October 1945, President Ho Chi Mingh accept for popular education of the Masses and for the eradication of illiteracy throughout the country within one year. The Vietnamese campaign began in 1945 with three interrelated tasks: registering students, mobilising personal and materials resources and designing administrative structures. In the space of a year 1945-46, 2.5 million became literate. By 1961, illiteracy was practically eradicated in the high lands. By December 1977, illiteracy had been eliminated among working people below 50 years old. In the mountain the age limit was 40 for both men and women. The campaign ended officially in March 1978.

When the people's Republic of China was established on October 1st 1949, illiteracy rate were very high, 85 percent in urban areas and 95 percent in the rural areas. In 1950, Government vowed to make 200 million people literate between the age-group 18-40 within five to seven years. The task was huge and time too short. In spite of its ups and downs, anti-illiteracy work received considerable success. Over 100 million illiterates between the age of 14 and 45 were made literate before 1966 and another 37.7 million after 1966. China's anti illiteracy efforts are clearly the greatest experiment in Mass Education in history.

One of the most widely known the Cuban Mass Literacy Campaigns which still inspire and challenge political leaders and literacy education in all parts of the world, was announced by Fidel Castro during his address to the General Assembly of the United Nations on 20 September 1960. The students acquired a new close consciousness, the girls learned a new identy an important first step towards the liberation of women in Cuba and in due course girls and boys alike supplied the nation with the essential party cardres, administrators, technicians and teachers, At the request of the Government, the Federation of Cuban women and committee for the Defence of the Revolution carried out a massive effort aimed at recruiting housewives as learners. They also served as literacy teachers, bringing many women into the learning process.

Slowly but surely and systematic under the Burma Socialist Programme part, the country rooted out literacy in a unique way. The first Literacy campaign was launched in 1904 as a pilot project. After intensive experiment during 1966-68 a new strategy for literacy promotion was adopted and a long term plan was approved in 1969. in the early 1980s literacy rate was reduced by some 10 percent to 30 percent of the population.

The Brazillian Literacy Movement (MOBRAL) was proclaimed on 8th September, 1967 to coincide with International Literacy Day. Today MOBRAL is a familiar name to Literacy workers throughout the world. The nationwide Mass Literacy Campaign of the United Republic of Tanzania was launched in September 1971. When Julius K. Nyerere emergedas leader of the nation, he had a coherent vision for his country, a clear cut developmental idology and there will be implemented his vision with the participation of the people. In August 1975, the illiteracy rate was 67 percent, in 1981, the rate had been lowered to 21 percent among the ranger group.

The literacy Campaign in Somali involved in two phases the Urban Literacy Campaign and the Rural Literacy Campaign. The complexity of the rural phase was the nature of population that had to be served. Each country must work out its Literacy Campaigns according to its own needs and circumstances. However, there is no harm in drawing lesson and inspirations from the countries listed in a aforesaid pages.

Historical experience suggests that a massive campaign which targets the overwhelming majority of adult non-literates, and more important, seeks to involve the entire population in a national efforts, is a must, especially for countries like India with a large non - literate population.

While political ideologies as well as conceptions of literacy have differed from one literacy campaign to another, strong commitment to the eradication of illiteracy on the part of the political leadership of the country has been indispensable to the success of every campaign.

Summing up the experience of mass campaigns for literacy the world over, one can say that they have generally taken place in a context of decisive transformations in the larger socio - economic spheres, political commitment and a conception of literacy that is merely functional but emphasis the inherent potential of literacy for liberation. Besides, for the success of such campaigns to be sustained, universalisation of schooling and committed implementation of carefully planned post - literacy and continuing education campaigns are crucial.

KERALA MODEL FOR TOTAL LITERACY

In the past century itself Travancore was considered a 'progressive' model state in British India in terms of the achievements in the fields of land, administration and education. In the most recent decades, Kerala has made significant progress particularly in those aspects which influence the physical quality of life. Till the establishment of the British hegemony and even during the first half of the nineteeth century Kerala society remained under determining aspects of caste system. The largely agrarian economy of Travancore has a hierorchical structure. In this set up, Facilities available for education for each community or group corresponded to their respective social status. Higher education especially in the Vedas in Sanskrit was a monopoly of the Brahmins and was patronised and supported by that royalty. However, educational facilities were available for all the socially provileged sections of the society. In contrast, vast sections of the society belonging to depressed communities did not have facilities for education and remained by and large illiterate.

For back in 1817, when the then Princes of the erstwhile Travancore State declared that expenditure on education will be fully met from state exchequer, the seeds of educational advancement in the state were sown. The starting of English schools in 1834 and tireless work of social reformers - Sri Narayana Guru, Chattampi Swamiji, Mannathu Padmanabhan, Ayyankali, Kumaran Asan, R. Sankar etc. In the field of eradication of illiteracy, the establishment of night schools during the pre-independence period was the first step. The starting of rural libraries and the formation of a movement in 1945 with 47 libraries was the first step in this direction.

During the Post-Independence period, there had taken place substantial progress in literacy and educational atainments of the population. Socially backward sections have also made considerable progress. However, the pace of educational development of these sections was low. In the last two decades, the literacy rate in the state increased for 60.4 in 1971 to 70.4 in 1981 and further to 90.6 in 1991; that of Scheduled Castes was 40.2, 56.0 and 79.7 percentages and of scheduled Tribes was 25.7. 31.8 and 57.2 percentages respectively during this period.

The formation of a Writers Co-operative Society (WCS) paved the way for boosting book production and thereby reading habits of people in Kerala. Under the Farmer's Functional Literacy Programme, 20 literacy centres were launched by the kerala Gradhasala Sangham. The Sangham in 1975 got the honourable mention for Krupskaya Award. Kerala Association for Non-formal Education and Development) (KANFED). was established in June 1977 as an offshoot of the Kerala Grandhasala Sangham and the State Literacy Council.

KANFED also began organising model literacy centres and continuing education centres in various parts of the State with the help of German Adult Education Association (DVV). At the time of the launching of National Adult Education Programme (NAEP), Kerala had already gone far ahead of other Indian States in regard to literacy percentage of both males and females. Kerala Sastra Shitya Parishad (KSSP) also did yeoman service in spreading scientific temper and consequently liteacy, awareness etc. were also offered to people through street dramas, science quizes, exhibition, publications of scientific literature etc.

The first total literacy campaign in the voluntary sector was launched by KANFED in Eyhome village of Kannur District. It was a great success. In Kottayam Muncipal area, TLC was launched by the Collector, Municipal Officials and the M.G. University NSS Unit. Consequent on the success of the TLC in Kottayam. Ernakulam District came forward to launch a massive, time bound programme all over the district, which had 1.86 lakhs illiterates.

KSSP and KANFED were in the forefront along with Government Officials. Awareness was created among the people through corner meetings, padayatra, cultural programmes etc. The illiterates were identified through a day's survey, covering all age groups. The age range covered was 6 to 60 years. Besides, NSV's and NSS volunteers, local volunteers were also located and given necessary training. Teaching learning materials were procured and distributed. The Management Information System launched also worked efficiently. Corrective measures were adopted wherever found necessary.

On 4 February, 1990 the Ernakulam District was declared as the first 'fully literate' disrict in the country, more than 1.5 lakhs persons had been made literate by over 20,000 volunteers. Each volunteer had put in around 240 hours of work over a six-month period. The Ernakulam TLC had unique features arising from the specific socio-economic and cultural millieu of the district. Soon after the success of Ernakulam Campaign, the all Kerala campaign called "Akshara Keralam" (Literate Kerala) was launched. On 18 April, 1991, Kerala was declared the first `totally literate state' in the country.

The folk entertainers and street - theatre groups had drummed up enthusiasm throughout the district. Many learners were aged 40 to 60 and came from groups such as landless laboures, fishermen and road-stone breakers, tribes and women. The success of the Kerala campaign brought literacy experts from other parts of India to learn from it.

EXPERIENCES OF TLC IN INDIA

After Erakulam in Kerala, Pondicherry was the second region in India declared as "Total Literate" on 30 th November 1991. In Pondicherry, ten cultural troupes (Kala Jathas) travelled through the villages, popularising the message of literacy through more than 1500 performances. About 13,000 volunteers were mobilised and trained. The TlC generated mass awareness and sought to make the poorest conscious of their rights.

The response of women to the campaign was encouraging. The Puduvai Arivli Iyyakkam was branded as "anti-national" by the speaker of Pondicherry Assembly. There followed a flurry of accusations against the campaign. The literates were introduced to the working of the Government Offices and police stations. They were taught simple things-such as using their newly acquired skills to fill a First Information Report.

A prosperous but populous district of West Bengal, Burdwan launched its TLC for 13.5 lakh illiterates in the 6-50 age group. The district is multi-religious and multi lingual. Its Urdu, Hindi and Oriya speaking learners, apart from Bengalis, have made the campaign both interesting and challenging. About 50 per cent of the target group belongs to the scheduled castes and the learners come from diverse occupational streams, among them landless labourers, bargadars (Share croppers) coal mine workers, industrial labour and the people in the unorganised sector.

Of the learners, 32 per cent were described as above average in relation to NLM norms, 46 per cent average and the rest below average. Though the percentage of learners reaching NLM norm is very high, most of them cannot be regarded as having reached a reasonable good standard in writing. It is too early to claim that the literacy drive has led to an improvement in the status of women and recognition of their rights in normal society. The immunisation programme has shown considerable progress in Burdwan during the campaign period.

The Nizamabad district in Andhra Pradesh was declared as 'Totally Literate' on 15 August, 1992 with an estimated 3.5 lakh learners having achieved levels in accordance with the NLM norms. Initially, low literacy rate, more Naxalite activities and *Beedi*–women workers were the main constraints in the district. But the Naxalite groups supported the TLC as a pro-people programme. The TLC in the district created great enthusiasm among the poor and among women, especially Muslim women. New awareness among the women has resulted the Anti-Arrack Movement in Nellore district of Andhra Pradesh.

Arun Ghosh visited some villages in rural Rajasthan to find out the working of literacy programme and observed that the feudal spirit is still very much alive in this part of the country. But even to break this feudal habit, the women need literacy and greater awareness. A great surprise feature was that for the 100 per cent literacy programme, the district has not asked for one single Naya Paise from either the State Government or the Central Government. The district authorities have decided that the people must be motivated to finance the campaign. This included purchase of couple of text books one slate and pencil for every student who volunteered to join literacy programme.

Sundaragarh Zilla Saksharata Samiti (SZSS) implemented TLC in Sundaragarh District of Orissa. Though, the district has a large tribal and scheduled caste population it has made 1.51 lakhs literate by TLC. Most of the villages were non-electrified and kerosene oil was not available in several places.

Narasinghpur district of Madhya pradesh is predominately agricultural, is a rich fertile tract of the Narmada valley and socially, is dominated by feudal system. The people who tried to come for the literacy classes were threatened and abused. Their note books, pens and pencils were snatched away. But the landless labourers and small farmers got orgnised and competed the TLC successfully.

The evaluation team nominated by the Government of India observed that most of the teachers are Government servants and they are bound by government orders. Their travelling allowance bills are also denied by the project officers. The funds are diverted to the Fducation Department. Apart from these motivational and organisational problems, the TLC of Narasinghpur faced the other problem of caste background teachers. Teachers were definitely hesitant to visit Harijan Mohallas or *Beedi*–worker's houses which belonged to 'low caste people'. The Muslim community were not interested in literacy due to the 'Purdah' system.

TLC IN TAMIL NADU

Tamil Nadu Literacy profile, as per the 1991 census, reveals that 63.72 per cent of the total population above 7 years of age are literate. Male and female literacy rates have been 74.88 per cent and 52.29 per cent respectively. Among the large States in then country. Tamil Nadu stands second next only to Kerala in literacy. Tamil Nadu could become the second major 'Totally Literate State' in the country.

In Tamil Nadu, based on the Kerala Experience, TLC had been implemented by the Non-Governmental Organisation, namely, Tamil Nadu Science Forum (TNSF) and State Resource Centre for Non-formal Education, Madras in most of the districts. The same method of organisational set up was followed as Central Programme Co-ordinator, Block co-ordinator, Assistant Block Co-ordinator, Master trainers, Resource persons and voluntary Instructors at the field level.

In order to findout the illiterate, 'One Day Survey' had been conducted in Tamil Nadu also. The BGVS and TNSF have conducted many Jatha and Booster Jathas to motivate the learners. Training of functionaries was organised at convenient places as residential programme inviting state level experts; resource persons. The MIS also follwoed to monitor the programme in Tamil Nadu. The unique features of Kerala Model is followed in all aspects of the TLC in Tamil Nadu. But in Tamil nadu, TLC include the priority group (15-35 years) according to the NLM, but in Kerala model it was 6-60 years and it tries to ensure 'Education For All'.

In Tamil Nadu, the proposal is to achieve cent percent literacy among the age group 15-35 before the end of 1994. Therefore, three phased total literacy campaign strategy has drawn up. During the first phase, 1991-92, seven disricts, namely. Pudukottai, Pasumpon, Kamarajar, Tirunelveli Kattabomman, Kanyakumari, Madurai, North Arcot

Ambadkar have been covered under total literacy campaign for the benefit of 19.94 lakhs of illiterates. Among the seven districts, Pudukootai, Kanyakumari, Pasumpan and Kamarajar district have been declared totally literate districts. In other districts, the campaign has been completed though the declaration has not been made.

With Kamarajar and Pasumpon making the initial break through, other districts followed in rapid succession. Even while the TLCS of the different districts have several common elements, based as they are on a common underlying model, each TLC has its own very distinctive characteristics. The total literacy campaign of Kamarajar district has become nationaly known precisely for certain rather unique features. Set in one of the most back ward districts - especially with regard to rural female literacy - the campaign brokes new ground, and became something of a model to many TLCS elsewhere in the state and in country.

During 1992-93, the second phase of the campaign has been started for the benefit of 26.50 lakhs of illiterates in six districts, namely, Ramanathapuram, Coimbatore, Nagapatinam, Quaid - E - Millath, Dindigul Anna, Periyar and Salem District. The third phase campaign are proposed to cover the 37.54 lakhs of illiterates. The campaign was commenced during the period 1993-94 and 1994-95 in the remaining districts, namely, Chengai MGR, Tiruvannamalai, Sambuvarayar, Nilgiris, Trichy, Chidambaranar, Thanjavur, South Arcot, Dharamapuri and Madras.

With regard to the financial achievements of TLC in Tamil Nadu, during phase-I, literacy campaign had utilised a total of Rs.1228.37 lakhs. Normaly, the Central Government has provided 2/3 of the total cost of the approved amount for the campaign. During the second phase period, the total amount released for the six districts was Rs.703 lakhs. But for the phase - III campaign in Tamil Nadu, Rs.2440.10 lakhs have approved for the campaign in a district.

During the period from 1991-92 to 1994-95, 64.76 percent of the total sanctioned amount was utilised for the TLC in Tamil Nadu. The total amount sanctioned for the campaign for the five year period was Rs.5355.45 lakhs. The amount utilised upto 1995-96 was

Rs.3468.13 lakhs. The remaining amount will be utilised during the post literacy campaign period in Tamil Nadu.

Good efforts have been made in the beginning by the several agencies such as Tamil Nadu Science Forum, the State Resource Centre for Non-Formal Education, the Directorate of Adult and Non-Formal Education and the Tamil Nadu Board of Continuing Education. Several 'Jathas' have been conducted by Bharat Gyan Vigyan Samiti (BGVS) to motivate illiterates and create awareness and urge among the educated to come forward to teach.

At present, in Tamil Nadu, the TLCs are implemented in 20 districts, Kamarajar, Pasumpon, Pudukottai and Kanyakumari districts were declared as 'totally literate' districts and they have entered the post-literacy phase. North Arcot, Nellai Kattabomman, Madurai and Ramanad districts are to be announced shortly as totally literate districts. The campaign are in the initial stages in Dindigul. Anna, Coimbatore, Nagapattinam Quad-e-Milleth and Periyar districts.

TLC IN KAMARAJAR DISTRICT

On 14 April 1991, the Tamil New year day, the TLC was launched with a mega convention and rally in Kamarajar District of Tamil Nadu. The Campaign was undertaken by the Kamarajar District Arivoli Iyakkam to cover more than 1.75 lakh learners in the age group of 15-35 in the district.

The Kamarajar District Campaign has shown the way to other campaigns in environment building and motivation. Apart from the main Jatha and the Booster Jatha of 1044 and 1008 performances, many new strategies such as Arivoli Ratha Yathras, burning the effigy of 'Demon illiteracy', painted literacy slogans on Buffalo and elephants which were taken round the streets, have met with phenomenal results. Trees hung with letters and words and wall writings in many places have kept a literate movement. Further 'Arivoli Deepam', the monthly Radio Programme over All India Radio. Madurai and "Arivoli Azhaikkirathu" the monthly newsletter have been instruments of consolidation and reinforcement.

The TLC in the district created a new awareness among the common fold on the need for literacy in general and education for the children in particular. The District Collector conducted the regular classes for the learners at the "Kooraikundu" village centre. It created a link between the highest rung in the district administration and the common man.

The performance of the Kamarajar District TLC in fulfilling the objectives of NLM were analysed through the information gathered during the field visits and the findings of the survey in many literacy centres. The results of the survey are:

The campaign created the awareness about the national integration. One example in Sattur block, three village coordinators, Sidiq (Muslim). Somasundaram (Hindu). Chelladurai (Christian) jointly performed their literacy work in many villages.

A volunteer instructor says that only after joining as volunteer in the campaign, he could develop the character of patience and the art of persuasive speech.

In Sempatti Village of Aruppukottai Union, a leprosy women learner got benefits from the campaign and she was recognised as a friend without any hesitation in the village centre by other learners.

The survey shows that the 36 per cent of learners got the savings habits in post office through this campaign. The TLC in the district improve the 72 per cent of women learners and 91 per cent of the volunteer instructors in leadership qualities like speaking, problem solving, solving puzzles, imagination and creativity.

The study reveals some of the important problems in implementation of TLC in Kamarajar district of Tamil Nadu. They are discussed below:

1. 24 per cent of the village centres were conducted under street lights due to the non-availability of space in homes. In many villages, the illumination of street lights was very poor and the places were not suitable during the rainy and cold seasons.

2. Secondly, the rate of dropouts in the backward regions were raised due to the migration of agricultural labourers during the harvest period of 3 months from December to February.
3. Since 67 per cent of the volunteers were students, it is difficult to run the centres continuously during the period of examinations in schools and colleges.
4. Even after starting the teaching-learning phase in the campaign, 18 per cent of the village centres did not get the slates, books and other teaching materials in time.
5. Only 7 per cent of the women dropouts stated that the illiterate as well as the literate husbands were not willing to send their wives to the centres.
6. The match and fireworks industries in some regions provide the full time work for the adults and the children and also home work for the women in all days. the learners and volunteers in these regions must forego their earnings for learning.
7. The acute water problems during the summer period retards the performance of TLC centres in drought areas.
8. Since the 33 per cent of the dropout learners satisfied with the ability in reading and writing, after completing the lesson VI in Arivoli Deepam-1, the rate of dropouts was increased in campaign.

The study suggests the following measures for the successful implementation of the TLC in India:

1. The school buildings with lighting facilities may be used for the Campaign in the evenings.
2. All other voluntary organisations may be motivated to be involved in the campaign.
3. The learners may be motivated through employment oriented learning in TLC.
4. The trained women volunteers may be utilised for motivating the dropout learners and instructors, to reduce the dropout rate in the village centres.
5. The teaching-learning phase may be selected suitably keeping in view the harvest season while the agricultural labourers migrated from one place to another and the examination period in schools and colleges for utilising the student volunteers fully in the campaign.

6. The teaching materials must be supplied to the village centres before starting the teaching-learning phase.
7. The literacy centres may be started in each and every match and fire works industry and the NLM must take necessary steps to impart literacy to the workers without affecting their earnings.

2

DROP-OUTS IN TOTAL LITERACY CAMPAIGN

INTRODUCTION

Efforts at Non-formal and Adult Education have been quite persistent in India, irrespective of their quality or extensiveness. The centre-based approach has been in vogue in the field. However, success in such programmes of mass literacy has not been necessarily quite to the level expected during their execution. The objectives of National Literacy Mission (NLM) was to revising and strengthening the existing adult education programme in the country.

The Total Literacy Campaign (TLC) model was developed and launched in several districts in India.

In Kamarajar District Of Tamil Nadu, the teaching-learning phase was started from July 1991 with the object of covering more than 1.75 lakhs of leaners. Many learners dropped out after completing the first primer (Arivoli Deepam I) and finally the District Arivoli Iyakkam had achieved in imparting literacy to 1.53 lakhs of learners. Therefore, it is necessary to study the reasons for the dropouts among the learners in the TLC.

The socio-political and economic problems in rural economy are the basic constraints on the efforts at achieving total literacy. An attempt has been made to analyse the reasons for the dropouts in the Kamarajar District TLC of Tamil Nadu.

OBJECTIVES

The specific objectives of the study are :

i) to analyse the socio-economic profile of the learners and the volunteers involved in the TLC of Kamarajar District;
ii) to identify the dropout rate among the learners in various centres of the TLC;
iii) to study the socio-political and economic reasons for dropping out;
iv) to review the measures taken and the problems faced by the implementors to reduce the rate of dropouts among learners in this campaign; and
v) to make concrete suggestions for the success of TLC in reducing dropouts.

REVIEW OF LITERATURE

In order to throw some light on the experiences of the TLCS in some other states, a few studies are reviewed below:

A study conducted by Sadhna Saxena in Narsinghpur District, Andra Pradesh revealed that the constraints of the socio-political and the economic structure of our rural society may reduce the concept of total literacy to a myth, unless such societal barriers are broken down and overcome. We will be forced to define total literacy without including the inaccessible sections of the population.

The study report of Michael Tharakan of the Centre for Development Studies, Trivandrum reveals that folk entertainers and street-theater groups had drummed up enthusiasm throughout the district, and volunteers raised Ernakulam's literacy rate from 82 per cent to 96 per cent within a year. The response to an appeal for unpaid instructors was over-whelming.

The multi-religious and multi-lingual Burdwan District TLC was evaluated Mid term by three experts and they observed that though the percentage of learners reaching NLM norm was very high, most of them could be regarded as having reached a reasonably good standard in writing. There were interruptions in the learning process in Burdwan owing to their pre-occupation with sowing and harvesting, particularly in the multi crop-sowing areas, which require attention even during the evenings. In West Bengal, 11 per cent of centres had a dropout rate of as much as 50 per cent and about 78 per cent of centres had average attendance rate of more than 80 per cent.

Low literacy rate, Naxalite activities and women *beedi* workers were the main constraints in the Nizambad District of A.P. Later, the Naxalite groups supported the TLC as a pro-people programme. The location of literacy centres, the lack of experience of the volunteers and the lack of involvement of the *beedi* workers' trade unions in the TLC. acted as limits on its scope in the district.

Sundararaman of BGVS mentions in his book that failure to learn is one of the most common causes of dropouts. They fail to learn, because our volunteers are inadequately trained to teach the illiterate how to acquire reading, writing and numeracy skills; especially, the 'word' method required a lot of training inputs.

Sindargarh Zilla Saksharata Samiti (SZSS) in Sundargarh District of Orissa made 1.51 lakh people literate through the TLC. The main constraint was the nature of the district with large tribal and scheduled caste populations. Many villages were non-electrified, and there was non-availability of kerosene in several places.

In order to find out the causes of dropout among the volunteers in Kamarajar, Pasumpon and Pudikottai districts of Tamil Nadu, a study was conducted by Mr. Rajan of State Resource Centre for Non-Formal Education, Madras. The study found that even though the programme planned for each one to teach ten learners, the volunteers have enrolled more than ten learners. The non-cooperation of the learners, pre-occupation with other work, irregularity of the learners were the main causes for the volunteers dropping out of the programme.

METHODOLOGY

Primary and secondary data were collected for the present study. Secondary data were collected from the office records of the District Collector (President of Arrival Iyakkam) and from various reports.

Primary data were collected by conducting a field survey in this District under study. Kamarajar District was purposively selected for the study.

The Kamarajar District Arivoli Iyakkam has benefited from 100 Resource Persons, 1400 Master Trainers, 1700 odd village Coordinators, around 14,900 volunteer Instructors, 400 Jatha Artists. And on the full time side, there have been around 121 project staff at the Central, Block/Municipal and sub-project levels, coordinating the entire work.

The district comprises 11 Panchayat Unions (Rajapalayam, Srivilliputtur, Watrap, Venmbakottai, Sivakasi, Sattur, Virudhunagar, Kariapatti, Aruppukottai, Trichuly and Narikudi) and 6 Municiipalities (Aruppukottai, Sattur, Sivakasi, Virudhunagar, Rajapalayam, Srivilliputtur). The campaign was implemented in these 17 project areas (11 unions and 6 Municipalities).

The primary data were collected from both the implementors and the beneficiaries. A survey was conducted with the pre - tested questionnaire in all 17 projects. Of the total implementors, 5 Resource Persons, 30 Master Trainers, 25 odd village Coordinators, 5 Project Staff and 170 Volunteers (10 from each project) were selected at random for the survey. From the beneficiary side, 340 dropout learners (20 learners from each project) were also randomly selected. The 340 dropout learners, 170 volunteers and 46 part time and 19 full time staff were interviewed with pre-tested separate questionnaires.

LIMITATIONS

The survey was conducted between April and July 1993 which is part of the post literacy campaign period in the Kamarajar District. It is difficult to enumerate the drop out learners in the period of TLC. Care was taken by the trained research investigators to collect the primary data from the TLC dropout learners.

A PROFILE OF THE KAMARAJAR DISTRICT

Kamarajar District is situated in the Southern part of Tamil Nadu. It covers an area of 4220 square Kilometres. It is bound on the north by Madurai District, on the east by Pasumpon and Ramanathapuram districts, on the west by the Western Ghats and on the south by Chidambaranar and Nellai Kattabomman districts.

The North east Monsoon period from October to December is the main rainy season in the district and gets annual rainfall of about 817.1 mm. The soil type of the district is black soil. The run off in these soil may vary from 20 per cent to 50 per cent depending upon the rainfall and gradient.

The total population of this district, according to 1991 census, is 16,40,907 persons. Of this 8,19,633 are men and the remaining 8,21,274 are women. Of these, 11,42,038 persons belong to the rural sector, and only 4,98,869 persons are from the urban sector. The SC/ST population cover 16 per cent of the total population.

The literacy rate, according to 1991 census is 41.5 percent. The educational institutions in the district are 1167 elementary schools, 65 High schools, 67 Higher secondary schools, 8 Arts Colleges, 2 Engineering Colleges, 8 Polytechnics, 1 Industrial Training Institutes.

The total labour force in the district is of 7,75,821 persons which is 47.28 per cent to the total population. Of the total labour force, 66.66 cent are engaged in the agricultural sector. The remaining 33.34 per cent are engaged in cottage, household industries, trade and commerce and other activities such as mining, quarrying, construction, transport, storage, communication etc.

There are 49 large scale industries, 438 small scale industries, 287 tiny sector sheds, and 34,139 rural and cottage industries in the district. The large scale industries are textile mills, cement, paper, printing, chemicals etc. A large number of small scale industrial units are engaged in the production of safety matches and fire works. The cottage industries are, handloom weaving, palmgur making, pottery, brick making and cottage match works.

All the villages in the district cannot claim to have drinking water facilities. Power supply and educational facilities are available in 98.3 per cent and 88.2 per cent of the villages respectively. 56.8 per cent of the villages in the district are accessible by pucca roads. Marketing, medical and post and telegraph facilities are available only in 3.3 per cent, 19.5 per cent and 34.9 per cent of the villages respectively.

Based on the above said profile of Kamarajar districts, the Total Literacy Campaign (Arivoli Iyakkam) was implemented successfully in this district.

GENERAL CHARACTERISTICS OF THE RESPONDENTS

It is necessary to consider the personal, socio-economic and psychological profile of the learners and volunteers for successful implementation of the Arivoli Iyakkam (TLC) by the project staff and the people. In this section, the socio-economic characteristics of the respondent are examined on the basis of the primary data collected for the study. In order to compare the implementation of the campaign, the study district was grouped as Panchayat union project area and Municipal project area.

Age wise classification of the respondents

The Kamarajar District Arivoli Iyakkam was implemented among learners of the 15-35 age group. The age wise classification of the 340 learners (20 learners from each projects) and 170 volunteers (10 volunteers from each project) are presented in Table-1. It is inferred from Table-1 that the campaign has covered 69.41 per cent (236 learners) of the targeted group (15-35 age) of learners, 14.12 per cent below 15 learners and 16.47 per cent. Above 35 learners in the district, 83.53 per cent (142) of 15-35 age group volunteers, 5.29 per cent (9) of volunteers below the age of 15 and 11.18 per cent of volunteers above 35 have be involved in the campaign. Mainly learners and volunteers are above 15.35 mainly participated in the total literacy campaign of the district.

TABLE - 1:
Age wise distribution of Sample Respondents

Age	Learners Union	Munici-pality	Total	Volunteers Union	Munici-pality	Total
Below 15	44	4	48 (14.12)	7	2	9 (5.29)
15-35	142	94	236 (69.41)	91	51	142 (83.53)
Above 35	34	22	56 (16.47)	12	7	19 (11.18)
Total	220	120	360 (100)	110	60	170 (100)

Source : Computed form primary data.
Note : Figures within parenthesis denote percentage.

Sex wise distribution

Women actively participated in the Kamarajar District TLC. The sex wise distribution of the sample respondents are exhibit in Table-2. Of the total 340 sample learners 269 (79.12 percent) are female and 71 (20.88 percent) are male. Among volunteers, 79 (45.47 per cent) are male and 91 (53.53 per cent) are female. The table also reveals that women learners are higher in both union and municipal areas but the male volunteers in the union areas and female volunteers in the Municipal areas participated in large number.

TABLE - 2 :
Sex wise Distribution of the Sample Respondents

Category	Learners			Volunteers		
	Union	Munici-pality	Total	Union	Munici-pality	Total
Male	55 (25.0)	16 (13.33)	71 (20.88)	67 (60.91)	12 (20.0)	79 (46.47)
Female	165 (75.0)	104 (86.67)	269 (79.12)	13 (39.09)	48 (80.0)	91 (53.53)
Total	220 (100.0)	120 (100.0)	340 (100.0)	110 (100.0)	60 (100.0)	170 (100.0)

Source : Computed from primary data.
Note : Figures within parenthesis denote percentage.

Marital Status

The marital status of the sample respondents are given in Table-3. It is clear from the table that of the total learner respondents, the married, the unmarried and widowers are 177 (52.06 per cent), 156 (45.88 per cent) and 7 (2.06 per cent) respectively. There are 47 (27.65 per cent) married volunteers, 104 (61.18 per cent) unmarried volunteers and 19 (11.17 per cent) widowers among the sample instructors in the district. The study reveals that a large number of married learners and unmarried volunteers had involved in the TLC of the district.

TABLE - 3 :
Marital Status of the Sample Respondents

Category	Learners			Volunteers		
	Union	Munici-pality	Total	Union	Munici-pality	Total
Married	91	86	177 (52.06)	29	18	47 (27.65)
Unmarried	124	32	156 (45.88)	70	34	104 (61.18)
widow/ widower	5	2	7 (2.06)	11	8	19 (11.17)
Total	220	120	340	110	60	170

Source : Computed from primary data.
Note : Figures with in parenthesis denote percentage.

Caste

In order to understand the problem of drop-outs in TLC, it is necessary to study the caste wise participation of the learners and volunteers in the district. The caste wise distribution of the sample respondents are presented in Table-4.

It is clear from table-4, of the total learner respondents, 131 (38.53 percent) learners belong to the scheduled caste/tribe, and 121 (35.59 per cent) belong to the backward class. It shows that the highest number of SC/ST and BC volunteers are involved in the campaign. 48.24 per cent (82) of BC volunteers and 27.06 per cent (46) of SC/

ST volunteers of the total sample volunteer respondents have participated. In the case of SC/ST and FC groups, volunteers availability is lower than in other castes.

TABLE-4 :
Caste wise Distribution of the Sample Respondents

Category	Learners			Volunteers			Learner & volunteer Ratio
	Union	Munici-pality	Total	Union	Munici-pality	Total	
Forward	3	12	15 (4.41)	3	–	3 (1.76)	7.5:3
Backward	52	69	121 (35.59)	41	41	82 (48.24)	60.5:82
Most Backward	57	16	73	35	4	39	36.5:39
Scheduled Caste/ Scheduled Tribes	108	23	131	31	15	46	65.5:46
Total	220	120	340 (100)	110	60	170 (100)	1:1

Source : Computed from primary data.
Note : Figures within parenthesis denote percentage.

Occupation of the Learners and Volunteer Instructors

Agriculture and some small scale industries like Matches, Fire works etc. dominate the study district. The occupation wise distribution of the sample respondents is given in table-5.

TABLES-5:
Occupation wise Distribution of Sample Respondents.ls1

Occupation	Learners			Volunteers		
	Union	Munici-pality	Total	Union	Munici-pality	Total
Government Servants	-	3	3 (0.88)	6	1	7 (4.12)
Farmers	59	14	73 (21.47)	4	1	5 (2.94)
Business/ Track	9	21	30 (8.82)	5	3	8 (4.71)
Cooly	151	80	231 (67.95)	28	12	40 (23.53)
Unemployed	1	2	3 (0.88)	19	29	48 (28.24)
Students	-	-	-	48	14	62 (36.47)
Total	220	120	340 (100)	110	60	170 (100)

Source : Computed from primary data.
Note : Figures with in parenthesis denote percentage.

Table-5 reveals that 67.95 per cent (231) of the total sample learner respondents are cooly workers (agricultural and non-agricultural) and the rest 32.05 per cent of learners, are farmers, businessmen, government servants and unemployed persons in the district. The study also reveals that a large number of students (36.47) percent, unemployed person (28.24 per cent) and cooly workers (23.53 per cent) are actively involved in the campaign.

Educational level

The learners enrolled in the Kamarajar District TLC might have studied in schools during their childhood days. The educational status of the sample learners are exhibited in Table-6. From the table, it is clear that 53.82 per cent of the learners had already attended schools and that the average number of years of attendance in schools is 2.51. 46.18 per cent of the sample learner respondents are totally illiterate.

The volunteers education status is given in Table-7. In the case of volunteers education, the 87.06 per cent of the volunteer respondents have studied above standard VIII and the rest, 12.94 per cent of volunteers, have below standard VIII education. In order to study the relationship between education of householders and the learners. The educational level of householder is analysed in Table-8. The study found that of the total learner respondents, 168 (49.41 per cent) householders are illiterate, and only a meagre portion of householders (5.88 per cent) has studied above the usual levels of schools education.

TABLE-6 :
Education Status of the sample Learners

Area	No. of learners attending schools during their childhood days				Total
	Illiterate	upto III std.	III to V std.	Total	
Union	98	97	25	122	220
Municipality	59	49	12	61	120
District	157 (46.18)	146	37	183 (53.82)	340

Source : Computed from primary data.
Note : Figures within parenthesis denotes percentages.

TABLE-7:
Educational Status of the sample volunteers

Level of Education	Union	Municipality	Total
Upto VII std.	15	7	22(12.94)
VII-XII std.	48	29	77 (45.29)
Above School level	47	24	71 (41.77)
Total	110	60	170 (100)

Source : Computed from primary data.
Note : Figures within parenthesis denote percentage.

TABLE-8:
Educational Status of the Head of the Learner's household

Area	Illiterate	upto VIII std.	VIII-XII std.	Above school level	Total
Union	117	62	30	11	220
Municipality	51	34	26	9	120
Districts	168 (46.41)	96 (28.24)	56 (16.47)	20 (5.88)	340 (100)

Source : Computed from primary data.
Note : Figures within parenthesis denote percentage.

Household Income

According to the Planning Commission of India, "Families of five members with an average annual income of Rs.6,400/- and below are classified as poverty families". The average annual income level of the sample respondents is presented in Table.9. The table reveals that more than 60 percent of the learners and the volunteer respondents live below the poverty line and 37.35 per cent (127) of learner respondents and 61 (35.88 per cent) volunteer respondents live above the poverty line. It is clear that a large number of learners and volunteer Instructos live below the poverty line.

TABLE-9:
Households Income Level of the Learners and the Volunteers

Category	No.of families earning below Rs.6400/-	No.of families earning above Rs.6400/-	Total
Learners			
Union	116	104	220
Municipality	97	23	120
Total Learners	213	127 (37.35)	340 (100)
Volunteers			
Union	70	40	110
Municipality	39	21	60
Total Volunteers	109 (64.12)	61 (35.88)	170 (100)

Source : Computed from primary data.
Note : Figures within parenthesis denote percentage.

Based on the above socio-economic profile of the respondents, the successful implementation of the Total Literacy Campaign in Kamarajar district has been analysed.

DROP-OUTS IN KAMARAJAR DISTRICT TOTAL LITERACY CAMPAIGN

The TLC was undertaken by the Kamarajar District Arivoli Iyakkam from April 1991 to cover more than 1.75 lakhs learners in the age group of 15-35 in the district. After completing the preparatory phase, the teaching phase was implemented during the period from October 1991 to June 1992. The Iyakkam succeeded in making literate 1.53 lakh persons, when the declaration was made.

Volunteer instructors and learners were enrolled in the campaign very actively at first. For many reasons, a certain percentage of the learners as well as the volunteers dropped out of the campaign. This section analyses the rate of dropout of learners, the reasons for learners dropping out and various suggestions for reducing dropout among learners in the Kamarajar District TLC.

Awareness of the TLC

In order to create awareness of the TLC among the volunteer instructors and the learners, the Arivoli Iyakkam conducted many convention, 1008 performances by 14 Kala Jatha troupes, rallies and procession in the district. The learners' participation in the campaign's various aspects is exhibited in Table-10.

TABLE-10 :
Awareness of TLC among the learners

Area	Kala Jatha	Friends	Volunteers	Advertise-ments	Total
Union	58	19	134	9	220
Municipality	19	12	87	2	120
Total	77 (22.65)	31 (9.12)	221 (65.0)	11 (3.23)	340 (100)

Source : Computed from primary data.
Note : Figures with parenthesis indicate percentage.

Table-10 thus reveals that 65 per cent (221) of learners respondents came to know about the campaign through the volunteer instructors. It shows the active participation of the volunteers in the campaign during the pre-teaching phase. The Kala Jatha has created awareness among 22.65 per cent of sample respondents. Advertisements through radio, T.V and friends influenced learners only to the extent of 3.23 per cent and 9.12 per cent respectively.

Expectations of the Learners in joining the campaign

The aims and reasons of the learners in joining the TLC in Kamarajar District are summarised in Table-1. The study reveals that 67.94 (231) per cent of the sample learner respondents got enrolled in the TLC to practice how to sign and to read distinction boards on buses and cinema wall posters. 16.47(56) percent of the sample learners came to the TLC centres owing to the compulsion of the Volunteer Instructors. 28 learners (8.24 per cent) participated in the campaign to regain and strengthen what they studied at school in their childhood days. The rest, viz, 7.35 percent (25) of the learner respondents aimed at real education under this campaign.

TABLE-11:
Expectations of the sample learner respondents

S.No.	Opinion of the learners	No.of	learners
1.	Practice to learn signature	129	(37.94)
2.	To read the bus boards, cinema poster etc.	102	(30.0)
3.	Compulsion of volunteers	56	(16.47)
4.	To have real education and knowledge	25	(7.35)
5.	To recollect the study at schools in beginning	17	(5.0)
6.	Others	11	(3.24)
	Total	340	

Source: computed from primary data.
Note : Figures within parenthesis denotes percentages.

TLC Centres

During the teaching phase in the Kamarajar District Campaign from October 1991 to June 1992, nearly 14,900 centres were opened in the villages and in the Municipal wards to give practice to the learners in writing and reading. The location of the centres is given in Table.12.

Table-12 reveals that the highest percentage (33.24) of sample learner respondents attended the street light centres while 31.76 per cent of learners attended centres in the houses of Volunteer Instructors. The rest, 35 per cent (19) learners, attended the centres in school buildings, community hall, and noon-meal centres.

TABLE-12 :
TLC Centres in the Districts
(No.of sample learners attending centres)

Area	House	Street light	School building	Community Hall	Noon-meal Centre	Total
Union	53	85	26	43	13	220
Municipality	55	28	6	27	4	120
District	108 (31.76)	113 (33.24)	32 (9.41)	70 (20.59)	17 (5.0)	340 (100)

Source : Computed from primary data.
Note : Figures within parenthesis denote percentage.

The study found that only 7 percent of the sample learners studied between 5 and 6.30 in the evening. Such centres were generally conducted by school going students. The largest number (93 per cent) of learners studied in the night that is from 7.30 to 9 which suited both the learners and the volunteer Instructors.

The study also found that of the 170 sample volunteers more than 60 per cent conducted classes on 4 to 6 days a week, while 24 per cent of them conducted classes on 3 days a week and the rest, namely 16 per cent conducted classes for learners below 3 days in a week.

Dropouts learners in Kamarajar District TLC

The teaching campaign in the district started with the enrollment of 1.73 lakhs learners and 14,900 volunteers to teach part-I of the primer, Arivoli Deepam. The learners and instructors voluntarily involved themselves in this campaign. Data were collected from the volunteers to find out the rate of dropout among learners in the campaign. The findings are given in Table-13.

TABLE 13 :
Drop-out of learners of learners According to the view of the Volunteers

	No. of Learners enrolled			No. of Regularly attending			Dropout Learners			Rate of Dropout of learners		
	Male	Female	Total	Male	Female	Total	Male	Female	Total	Male	Female	Total
Union	477 (4.34)	963 (8.75)	1440 (13.09)	265 (2.41)	655 (5.95)	920 (7.46)	212 (1.93)	308 (2.8)	520 (5.64)	44.44	31.98	36.11
Municipality	148 (2.47)	758 (12.63)	906 (15.01)	80 (1.33)	473 (7.88)	553 (8.38)	68 (1.13)	285 (4.75)	353 (6.72)	45.95	37.60	37.21
District	625 (3.68)	1721 (10.12)	2346 (13.8)	345 (2.03)	1128 (5.75)	1473 (7.78)	280 (1.65)	593 (4.37)	873 (6.02)	44.8	31.98	36.11

Source: Computed from primary data.
Note: Figures within parenthesis denote average number of learners in a village ward centre.

TABLE-14:
Phases of Dropping out of learners

	No. of drop outs during the first 30 days of teaching period	No. of dropout among learners before completing the primers First	Second	Third	Total
Union	56	92	42	30	220
Municipality	49	41	18	12	120
District	105	133	60	42	340
	(30.88)	(39.12)	(17.65)	(12.35)	(100)

It is clear from the table-13 that the rate of dropout of learners in the district TLC is 37.21 and that the rate of dropout among male learners in higher (44.8) than that (34.46) among women learners according to the sample study. The average number of learners enrolled in a centre is 3.68 male, 10.12 female and those who regularly attended were 2.03 male and 5.75 female on an average. The view of the volunteers reveals that, of the total (6.02) dropout leaners in a centre, the occurrence was 1.65 among males and 4.37 among females on an average. The study found that the number of learners enrolling, and regularly attending are higher in the case of the female category and that the higher rate of dropouts is in the male category.

It is inferred from the Table-14 that a large portion of learners dropped out from the campaign during the first 30 days of teaching period (30.88 per cent) and before completing the first primer, Arivli Deepam-I (39.12 per cent). The dropouts are low among the sample learner respondents during the teaching of the second (17.65 per cent) and the Third Primers (12.35 per cent).

Reason for dropout among learners

In order to findout the reasons for the learners dropping out in the Kamarajar District TLC, data were collected separately from the Volunteer Instructors, the learners and the implementors like Central Programme Co-ordinator, Project Officers, Assistant project Officers, Master Trainers, Resource Persons and Village Co-ordinators. The district is dominated by agriculture and small scale industries like fire works, Match Industries etc. The reasons for dropouts among the learners according to the opinion of the learners are exhibited in Table-15.

TABLE-15 :

Opinion of the dropout learners about the reasons for dropout in TLC

S.No.	Reasons	No.of Learners	Percen-tage	Rank
1.	No suitable time	44	12.94	4
2.	Poor lighting and Lack of Accommodation	89	26.18	1
3.	Irregularity of Volunteers and functioning of the centre	31	9.12	6
4.	Tiredness of leaners after completing the wage earning work and domestic chore	48	14.12	3
5.	Migration of learners for wage earning	41	12.06	5
6.	Lack of interest in leaners to study	20	5.88	7
7.	After knowing how to sign	64	18.82	2
8.	Other reasons	3	0.88	8
		340	100.00	

Source : Computed from primary data.

The study found that of the total sample dropout learner respondents, 26.18 per cent (89) learners dropped out owing to poor lighting and accommodation in centres in the villages and wards. Another major reason is that the learners felt that it was enough how to sign their names owing to the non-availability to time for learners and their tiredness after completing wage-earning work and domestic chores 27.06 per cent (92) of the learner respondents dropped out of the campaign. Agricultural labourers in some specific areas of the district usually migrate for a few months to earn and income. 12.06 per cent (41) of the learner respondents could not attend classes on account of such migration. In some backward areas, non-availability of volunteers was yet another cause, and the centres did not function properly which led to 9.12 per cent (31) dropout among the sample learners of the campaign. The rest, i.e. 6.76 per cent of learner respondents, failed to attend classes for other reasons such as child care, lack of interest in studies, factory/farm owner's compulsion.

Suggestions to reduce the rate of dropout learners

The suggestions made by the learners in order to reduce the rate of dropout learners are given in Table-16. The Table reveals that 20 per cent (68) of the sample learners suggest provision of lighting and adequate space. It shows that the poor lighting and space affect the regular functioning of the centres. 14.41 per cent (49) of the sample learners expect the volunteers to conduct the classes regularly. 56 (16.47 per cent) economically backward class people want to get compensation for wage loss suffered because of their attendance in the TL classes. The working hours in some factories like matches, fire works, cotton textiles etc. could be reduced through Government orders in order to impart literacy in the TLC. The other suggestions by the sample learners are to give handicrafts training (5.59 per cent), organize culturally oriented activities in the centres (9.12 per cent), secure prior pemission from the employer and householder (7.06 per cent) etc.

TABLE-16

Suggestions by Sample Dropout Learners to reduce the rate of dropouts

S.No.	Suggestions	Number of Learners responded	Percentage
1.	To give handicrafts Training	19	5.59
2.	To provide lighting facilities and near residence centres	68	20.00
3.	To make arrangements to conduct the classes by volunteers continuously	49	14.41
4.	To organize culturally oriented activities in the centres	31	9.12
5.	To get prior permission from the head of the household and the employer	24	7.06
6.	To take necessary action to reduce working hours	47	13.82
7.	To provide compensation for wage loss during the study hours	56	16.47
8.	To introduce the learners in the public village/ward festival meetings	14	4.12
9.	Meeting the learners regularly by the project staff	19	5.59
10.	Others	13	3.92
		340	100.00

Source : Computed from primary data.

Training for volunteer Instructors

Table-17 reveals that of the total 170 sample volunteers, 58 volunteers (34.12 per cent) had already got teaching experience before the TLC in the district. They had served in the National Adult Education programme (NAEP), Private Schools, Non-formal Education etc. The rest, namely, 112 volunteers (65.88 per cent), were involved in the campaign without any previous teaching experience.

TABLE-17
Teaching Experience of the Volunteers

Area	Number of volunteers with teaching experience before TLC					Number of volunteers without previous teaching experience	Total
	NAEP	Private Schools	Non-formal	others	Total		
Union	19	3	2	8	32 (29.09)	78 (70.91)	110
Municipality	6	4	1	15	26 (43.33)	34 (56.67)	60
	25	7	3	13	58 (43.12)	112 (65.88)	170

Source : Computed from primary data.
Note : Figures within parenthesis denote percentage.

For the successful implementation of the TLC in the district and for updating teaching skills of the volunteers, training was given in three stages at the Block/Municipality level. Before the introduction of each primer (Arivoli Deepam), training for the volunteers was given by Master Trainers of the TLC often also assisted by the Resource Persons. The attendance pattern of the sample volunteer Instructors at the training is presented in Table-18.

It is clear from Table-18 that the sample volunteers who did not receive any training is at the insignificant (8.82 per cent) level and that a large number of volunteers (91.18) attended the training programmes. Of the 155 sample volunteers who received training the numbers attending 1-3 days, 4-6 days and 7-9 days are 23 (14.84 per cent), 37 (23.87 per cent) and 95 (61.29 per cent) respectively.

TABLE-18
Sample Volunteers Attended Training programmes in the Campaign

Area	Number of volunteers who attended training				Number of volunteers who did not attend training owing to					Total
	1-3 days	4-6 days	7-9 days	Total	No communication	No time	Not necessarly	others	Total	
Union	16	22	61	99 (90.0)	2	7	-	2	11 (10.0)	110 (100.0)
Municipality	7	15	34	56 (53.33)	1	3	-	-	4 (6.64)	60 (100.0)

Source : Computed from primary data.
Note : Figures within parenthesis denote percentage.

The opinions of the volunteers about the training programmes under TLC are analysed in this study and it is found that the sample volunteers are satisfied with the training period, supply of materials and the suggestion for reducing dropouts learners. The sample volunteer respondents are not satisfied with the topics, discussion, creative thinking and training for reducing dropout learners. These are summarised in Table-19.

TABLE-19
Opinion of the sample volunteers about the training programmes in the TLC

S.No.	Item	No.of volunteers respondent Satisfied	Not satisfied	Total
1.	Period of Training	147	23	170
2.	Topics discussed	94	76	170
3.	Materials supplied	161	9	170
4.	Creative Thinking	21	149	170
5.	Training for reducing dropout learners	25	145	170
6.	Suggestions to enroll the dropout learners	152	18	170

Source : Computed from primary data.

Measures to Reduce the dropout learners

From the experience of the other TLC's the central programme co-ordinators suggest various measures to reduce the number of dropout learners. The measures taken by the volunteers are enlisted in Table-20.

TABLE - 20
Effective measures undertaken by the sample volunteer instructors to reduce the rate of dropouts in the Campaign.

	No. of volunteers undertaking more specific activities to reduce the rate of dropouts						
Area	Door canvassing & meeting personally	Light & other facilities	Jatha etc.	Committee for village	Learners meet	Others	Total
Union	37	21	14	16	12	10	110
Municipality	22	13	8	7	6	4	60
District	59 (34.71)	34 (20.00)	22 (12.94)	23 (13.53)	18 (10.5)	14 (8.24)	170 (100)

Source : Computed from primary data.
Note : Figures within parenthesis denote percentage.

Table-20 reveals that a majority of the sample volunteers undertook door canvassing and personal meeting to reduce the rate of dropouts learners in the campaign. The impact of providing lighting and others facilities to the learners also is found favorable in reducing the dropout rate. Other measures such as Exhibition, Jatha, Village, Committee, Learners meet etc. were generally undertaken by a modest number of sample volunteers in the campaign.

Opinion of the volunteers about the reasons for dropout learners

The reasons for dropouts among the learners according to the opinion of the volunteers are presented in Table-21:

TABLE-21 :
Opinion of the volunteers about the reasons for dropout learners in TLC

		Number of volunteers responding	Perce-ntage	Rank
1.	Poor Lighting and lack of Accommodation	36	21.18	1
2.	Low interest of the learners to study	19	11.17	4
3.	Inadequate supply of materials to the centres	9	5.29	7
4.	Non-suitability of Arivoli Deepam in practice	14	8.24	5
5.	Tiredness of learners after completing the wage earning work and domestic chores	32	18.82	2
6.	Irrelevance of learning books to their profession	12	7.06	6
7.	Restrictions for women in their houses	8	4.71	8
8.	Non availability and no suitable time	26	15.29	3
9.	Non-cooperation of Government officials and factory owners	7	4.12	9
10.	Others	7	4.12	10
	Total	170	100.00	

Source: Computed from primary data.

It is clear from the Table-21 that the main reasons for the dropout learners in the study district TLC according to the view of the volunteers are lack of adequate accommodation and lighting (21.18 per cent), tiredness of the learners after completing the works(18.82 percent) and the non - availability and no suitable time for the learners to study (15.29 per cent). More than 10 per cent of the sample volunteers viewed that low interest of the learners to study, no suitability of Arivoli Deepam in practice and irrelevance of learning books to their profession are also influence the learners to dropout from the TLC. The insignificant reasons for the dropout learners are inadequate supply of materials to the centres, restrictions for women in their houses and non-cooperation of Government officials and factory owners.

From Table-22, it is clear that the more effective suggestions for reducing the rate of dropout learners, in the opinion of the sample volunteers are efficient training to the volunteers to conduct the centres with cultural orientation (19.41 per cent), providing lights and other infrastructure to the learners (13.53 per cent), organising village committees such as women's committee, Youth Committee etc. (12.94 per cent) and suitable teaching/ learning time for learners (10.59 per cent). The less significant suggestions as incentives to learners, Door canvassing, Jatha Learners's Meet etc.

TABLE -22

Suggestions of volunteers to reduce Rate of Dropout learners

S.No.	Suggestions	Number of volunteers responding	Percentage
1.	Door canvassing by the volunteers	14	8.24
2.	Organising various committees	22	12.94
3.	Suitable teaching period for learners	18	10.59
4.	Exhibition and other Jatha programmes	11	6.47
5.	Providing lighting & Other facilities	23	13.53
6.	Frequent visits by project staff to the centre	8	4.71
7.	Co-operation of Government officials and factory owners	13	7.65
8.	Supply of Tiffen, Uniform, incentive etc. to the learners	14	8.24
9.	Efficient training to the volunteers to conduct the centres (culturally oriented)	33	19.41
10.	Learners' Meet	10	5.88
11.	Others	4	2.34
		170	100.00

Source : Computed from primary data.

Opinion of the Implementors about the Dropout among the learners in TLC

In order to findout the reasons for the dropout among the learners and suggestions to reduce the dropouts, data were collected from the 65 part/full time staff by adopting the interview method. The findings are summarised in this section.

Reasons for the dropout learners in Kamarajar District TLC According the opinion of the Implementors

The reasons for the dropping out of learners in the campaign vary from place to place.

The study found that in Tiruchuli and Narikudi Blocks, the learners migrated to other places to earn a livelihood from Brick industries at Manamadurai, and fire wood factories at Paramakudi.

In Aruppukottai and Sattur both in the Unions and the Municipalities the learners work in match factories from 3 a.m. to 7.30 p.m. Being tired after such work, they are not able to attend the TLC classes.

In Sivakasi and Sattur, both in the Unions and the Municipalities, the match, fire works owners restricted the attendance in TLC classes by providing home work to the worker learners.

In Srivilliputhur and Watrap areas, the teaching period (October to June) is the peak agricultural period. Owing to the shift system in textile mills at Rajapalayam, the learners dropped out of the campaign.

It is noted that a number of centres did not function owing to the non-availability of volunteers in Virudhunagar and Kariapatti. Poor lighting facilities in the villages and the wards, lack of interest of learners after learning how to sign, migration of workers, and unsuitable time are the main reasons for the dropping out of learners in the district.

Suggestions to reduce the rate of dropout learners

More than 74 per cent of the sample implementors in Kamarajar District suggested the following measures to reduce the rate of dropouts in TLC:

i) In order to distribute the work load of TLC, various committees such as village committee, youth committee, women's committee must be organised.

ii) Creative training through innovative method should be given to the volunteers as well as to the learners.
iii) Frequent learner's meet and volunteer's meet may motivate the dropout learners in the TLC.

The rest of the 26 per cent of sample implementors add the following measures for reducing the dropout learners.

a) Providing infrastructural facilities like lighting, accommodation etc.
b) Relaxation from the work and control of factory owners with the help of Government officials may be arranged to participate in the TLC.

SUMMARY AND CONCLUSION

The primary data collected from dropout learners, volunteer instructors, Resource persons, Assistant Project Officers, Project officers and Central Programme Coordinators are analysed and summarised below:

1. Of the 340 sample learners, 236 (69.41 percent) learners are in the targeted age group of 15-35 in this campaign.
2. The women learners constitute a higher number in both the Union and the Municipal areas, but in the matter of volunteers in the Union areas the men are larger in number while women volunteers dominate Municipal areas.
3. A large number of married learners (52.06 percent) and unmarried volunteers (61.18 per cent) involved themselves in the TLC of the district.
4. The level of illiteracy and learner's participation are higher in the case of SC/ST and B.C. in this campaign. In the case of SC/ST and F.C. groups, volunteer availability is lower than that in other groups.
5. Of the 340 sample learners, 67.95 per cent are the cooly (agricultural and non-agricultural) workers. A large number of student volunteers (36.47 per cent) have been actively involved in the campaign.
6. 46.18 per cent of the sample learners are totally illiterate and the rest, 53.82 per cent, have had some schooling in their childhood days and they were participated in the centre based approaches

like Adult Education Programme, Each one teach one and Non-formal Education. In the case of volunteers' education 87.06 per cent volunteer respondents have studied above standard VIII and the rest, 12.94 per cent, have the below standard VIII education.

7. More than 60 per cent of the dropout learners and volunteers live below the poverty line of Rs.6400 per year.
8. 65 per cent of learners got to know of the campaign through volunteer instructors. The Kala Jatha has created awareness among 22.65 per cent of the sample respondents.
9. Of the total learners, 67.94 per cent set the goal practicing how to sign and also reading the distinction boards on buses. Only 16.47 per cent came to the TLC centres on the compulsion of the volunteer instructors.
10. Of the learners who atended TLC centres, 108 did it at volunteer's houses (31.76 per cent), 113 under the street light (33.24 per cent), and 70 (20.59 per cent) in community halls and others locations.
11. The rate of dropout of learners in the campaign is 37.21. The dropout rate is higher in the male category (44.8) than in the female (34.46) category.
12. Of the 340 dropout learners, 30.88 per cent dropped out of the campaign during the first 30 days of teaching period, and 39.12 per cent dropped out before completing the first primer.
13 Of the 170 volunteers, 58 (34.12 per cent) volunteers had some previous teaching experience before TLC and the rest (112) entered without any teaching experience.
14. 91.18 per cent of volunteers attended the training programmes of the TLC. The volunteers are not satisfied with the topics discussed, creative thinking and training for reducing dropouts during the training programmes.
15. Most of the volunteers suggested the door canvassing (34.71 per cent) and providing light and other facilities (20.0 per cent) to reduce the rate of dropout among learners.
16. According to the opinion of the dropout learners, providing facilities, regular handling of classes by volunteers, reduction of work hours in factories and compensation for their wage loss are the suggestions for reducing the rate of dropout among learners.
17. The more effective suggestions for reducing the rate of dropout learners, in the opinion of volunteers and other implementors are (a) Efficient training for the volunteers to conduct the centres

with a strong cultural orientation (19.41 per cent), providing lighting and other facilities (13.53) per cent, (c) organising village youth committees, women committees (12.94 per cent) and (d) suitable teaching hours for learners (10.59 per cent).

It may be concluded that it is possible to reduce the rate of dropping out of learners in the TLC by improving the cultural oriented training Programme for volunteers, providing for creative activities for volunteers in the centres, arranging lighting facilities and shaping skilled volunteers for conducting the centres regularly. This will help the campaign to be successfully implemented in any district of our country.

3

TOTAL LITERACY CAMPAIGN ON SCHOOL ENROLMENT AND DROPOUTS

STATEMENT OF THE PROBLEM

Increased access to primary schools and reduced dropouts rate in India are the targets for elementary education in Eighth Plan (1990-95). The plan aims at universal enrolment of all children, including girls and persons beloning to SC/ST. Provision of primary schools for all children within one Kilometer of walking distance and facility of non-formal education is an important target. The plan also underlines the importance of reducing drop out rate between class I to V and I to VIII from the existing 46 per cent and 60 per cent to 20 per cent and 40 per cent respectively.

The NLM had taken efforts to motivate the parents for increasing school enrolment and reducing dropout rates through the TLC and Post-literacy Campaign (PLC). Some of the measures taken by the Union and State Governments to improve the school enrolment and retention are: Provision of incentives such as free text books, free uniforms, scholarships, mid day meals etc., community mobilisation to the need for literacy, appointment of women teachers, provision of day care centres to take care of young siblings, expansion of facility in schools through the scheme of operation Balckboard and provision of a network of centres for in-service and continuing education of school teachers by establishing District Institutes of Education and training, according to the Union government.

In India, an increasing number of girls are joining primary schools, with the number growing to 42.4 million in 1991-92 from 5.4 million in 1950-51. The All India School dropout rate has been higher among girl students than boys for the past three years though there has been a decrease in the overall dropout rate.

Tamil Nadu has a dropout rate of 20.32 at the primary school level against 44.37 which was the national dropout rate for 1990-91. The corresponding dropout rate for girls was 22.68 for Tamil Nadu against the all India rate of 47.61. At the primary school level, Tamil Nadu's dropout rate was the third lowest during the three years (1990-91 to 1992-93) with only Goa and Kerala performing better than Tamil Nadu.

In total literacy districts, there has been an increase in the school enrolment rates. A report of the District Collector/President of Arivoli Iyakkam showed that after the implementation of TLC in Kamarajar district, there is considerable increase in school enrolment in the year 1992-93 and dropout from schools is minimum. This is significant because the district has a number of child labour working in match and fire works industries. Therefore, it is necessary to study the impact of TLC in Kamarajar district. The present study attempts to analyse the impact of TLC in the school enrolment and dropouts from schools in Kamarajar District of Tamil Nadu state.

OBJECTIVES OF THE STUDY:

The specific objectives of the study are:

1. to analyse the student enrolment and strength in primary schools in Kamarajar district before and after implementation of TLC i.e. from 1990-91 to 1993-94.
2. to find the rate of dropout among school children from I standard to V standard for the same period (1990-91 to 1993-94) in the district; and
3. to make concrete suggestions to raise the school enrolment and retention rate through TLC.

REVIEW OF LITERATURE:

This section reviews some of the studies relating to the causes for dropouts and suggestions for raising the enrolment and retention rate in primary schools.

The findings of the study conducted by Central Institute of Research and Training in Co-operation (1975) are that it is largely poverty that forces SC children to give up school and hostility towards the advance of harijans, discrimination practiced by teachers, illtreatment by classmates and the distance between the home and the school are other reasons mentioned.

Reddy (1977) found that while the primary school educated father would send his son to school, it would normally need a post primary education for a father to be convinced to need to educate his daughter.

AID Research and Development Abstracts (1977) revealed that one means of achieving an increase in school attendance could be expansion of adult literacy progrmmes in India. If parents perceive a personal benefit from literacy, they are also likely to encourage their children to attend school.

A pilot project was carried out by Rengarajan (1977) in Tamil Nadu to identify the nature and causes of dropouts and to prepare a functional model for imparting education to the dropouts. The study revealed that the personality of the teacher is a crucial factor. To accommodate the specific characteristics of the seasonally working rural clientele, the flexibility of the system is importance.

Some case studies of UNESCO (1984) revealed that wastage due to dropping out and repetition is a problem in many of the school systems in the country. Its intensity varies from region to region and it is usually associated with differential rates of dropout and stagnation by sex wherein girls lag behind boys and by caste wherein the scheduled castes lag behind the non-scheduled castes. It is also closely associated with the socio-economic conditions, where poverty is greatest.

Seetharamu and Usha Devi (1985) analysed in five different regions in India and found that 20.1 percent for the sample dropouts are engaged in paid work. Among them 14.5 per cent are engaged in paid agricultural work and 5.6 per cent in non-agricultural work.

DESIGN OF THE STUDY

Kamarajar District of Tamil Nadu was purposively selected for the study because the district tops in the matter of both rural (50.2), urban (46.07) main workes and child workers in match and fireworks industries. The district has 1167 primary schools, 162 middle schools, 67 high schools, and 71 higher secondary schools. For the administrative convenience, the district was divided into three educational divisions, namely, Aruppukkottai, Virudhunagar and Sivakasi. The study was conducted in the Aruppukkottai Division.

Secondary data and primary data were used for the analysis of present study. Secondary data regarding the school details, strength of teachers, strength of students etc., were collected from the office records of Chief Educational Officer, Virudhunagar, District Educational Officers, Aruppukkottai Division and Inspector of Girls Schools, Virudhunagar. Primary data was collected from the primary school headmasters through interview method in the Aruppukkottai Educational Division of Kamarajar District.

After selecting the study District and the Aruppukkottai Educational Division, the two blocks were selected on the basis of economic development of the blocks. The Aruppukkottai division includes 5 blocks, namaly, Trichuly, Narikkudi, Aruppukkottai, Sattur and Kariapatti. Of the 5 blocks, 2 blocks - Trichuly and Aruppukkottai were selected, since these two blocks are economically developed blocks.

Both the sample blocks are producing a large amount of paddy, cotton, groundnut, and other cereals and pulses. A major portion of employment opportunities are also provided by the agricultural and non-agricultural works such as rice mill, oil mill, fire works, match works, handloom, powerloom and textile industries. The study assumes that the campaign could effectively implemented in these developed blocks due to the availability of socio-economic facilities.

The study aims to collect the primary data from the all 151 schools in two blocks. Due to non-availability of records in schools, unwillingness of headmasters and the financial constraints to collect the data, the primary data were administered from 120 rural and TLC dominated schools. These 120 schools are considered as sample schools.

The pre-tested schedule used to enumerate the data from school headmasters include the socio-economic status of the school headmasters, school particulars, strength of teachers and students, school enrolment and drop-out students rate during the period from 1990-91 and 1993-94 and the opinion of the school headmasters about the performance of TLC in the motivation and awareness to parents. The collectd secondary and primary data is analysed by using the descriptive analysis.

The study covers the period of 4 years 1990-91 to 1993-94. The TLC was implemented in the Kamarajar District during the period 1991-92. In order ot compare the school enrolment and dropouts in primary schools before and after implementation of TLC, the study analysed the 4 years performance of the primary schools. The field survey was conducted with the school headmasters during the period of December 1993 to January 1994.

The 25.83 per cent of the sample school headmasters were participated in TLC as part time resource persons, project officers, block level co-ordinators, etc. Care was taken by the research investigators to enumerate the real factors without any bias and prejudice of the school headmasters.

RESULTS AND DISCUSSION

1. Schools in Aruppukkottai Division

Aruppukkottai Educational division administers 3 taluks (Trichuly, Aruppukkottai and Sattur) school administration and it covers the 5 blocks. The school details of this division are presented in Table 1 and 2.

TABLE 1

School details in Aruppukkottai Division (No.of Schools)

S.No.	Schools	Govern-ment	Panchayat/ Municipal	Private Aided	Private Unaided	Total
1.	Primary Schools	3	323	109	-	435 (80.71)
2.	Middle Schools	-	39	22	-	61 (11.32)
3.	High Schools	17	-	3	1	21 (3.89)
4.	Higher Sec. Schools	13	9	-	-	22 (4.08)
	Total	33	371	134.	1	539 (100.0)

Note : Figures within parenthesis denotes percentages.
Source: Records of the Educational officer

TABLE-2

Primary and Middle Schools in Aruppukkottai Division

Sl.No.	Blocks	Government		Panchayat		Aided Private		Total		Total
		P	M	P	M	P	M	P	M	
1.	Aruppukkottai	-	-	6	6	26	5	87	11	98
2.	Kariapatti	-	-	70	9	28	4	98	13	111
3.	Trichy	1	-	39	2	24	7	64	9	73
4.	Narikudi	1	-	74	9	12	4	87	13	100
5.	Sathur	1	-	79	13	19	2	99	15	114
	Total	3	-	323	39	109	22	435	61	496

Note : P - Primary M - Middle
Source : Records of the Educatinal Officer.

The Aruppukkottai Division covers more than 80 per cent primary schools (435) of the total schools. Of the 435 primary schools, the panchayat union/municipalities admınister the 323 schools in this division. The domination of private aided schools are comparatively low in Aruppukottai Educational Division.

2. Students' strength in Aruppukkottai Division

The total strength of students in primary schools and middle schools of Aruppukkottai Division in 1993-94 are exhibited in Table-3. It is clear that the girls' enrollment in primary and middle school in this division is 48.7 per cent and 42.93 per cent respectively. These figures are higher than the national average of girls' enrollment in primary school (45.7 per cent) and middle school (37.73 percent).

The study found that, due to poor facilities in Panchayat union schools, the students strength was lower than the private aided schools i.e. 57.16 per cent of the students are studying in 109 private aided primary schools, whereas the 42.36 percent are studying in 323 panchayat union schools.

DATA COLLECTED FROM SCHOOL HEAD MASTERS

The data collected from head masters through interview method are analysed in this section.

1. Socio - Economic Status of Respondents

The socio-economic characteristics of the sample head masters of primary schools are illustrated in Table-4. The findings of the study are: (1) 56.67 percent of the sample head masters are above 50 years of age: (2) only 29.17 per cent of the respondents are female teachers in primary school: (3) more than 65 per cent of the head masters had completed SSLC and 20 per cent at the Master Dcgree Level: (4) 7.5 per cent of the head masters belong to the Scheduled Caste community and (5) more than 70 percent of the respondents got above 20 years of experience.

TABLE-3

Strength of students in primary school of Aruppukkottai Division (No. of students)

Category	Government School		Panchayat Municipality School		Private aided School		All Schools (percentage)		Total
	Rural	Urban	Rural	Urban	Rural	Urban	Rural	Urban	
Primary School									
Boys	172	-	13,300	1,218	8,010	12,882	21,482	14,100	35 (51.30)
Girls	160	-	13,701	1,162	7,103	11,652	20,964	12,814	33,778 (48.60)
Total	332	-	27,001	2,380	15,113	24,534	42,446	26,914	66,360 (100.00)
Middle School									
Boys	-	-	15,272	1,757	2,177	3,939	17,449	5,696	23,143 (57.07)
Girls	-	-	10,380	1,740	1,513	3,777	11,893	5,696	23,145 (42.93)
Total	-	-	25,652	3,497	3,690	7,716	29,342	11,213	40.555 (100.00)

Note: Figures with parenthesis denotes percentages.

TABLE - 4
Socio - Economic Status of Respondents (No.of Head Masters)

Area	Age (Years)		Sex		Education			community		Experience (Years)	
	Above 50	Below 50	Male	Female	SSLC	Gra duate	Post Gra duate	SC	Others	Above	Below
Trichyly	27	33	46	14	44	6	10	6	54	35	25
Aruppukkottai	41	19	39	21	36	9	15	3	57	57	3
	68 (56.67)	52 (43.33)	85 (7.83)	35 (29.17)	80 (66.67)	15 (12.5)	25 (20.33)	9 (7.5)	54 (92.5)	35 (76.67)	25 (23.33)

Note: Figures within parenthesis denotes percentages.

TABLE - 5
Details of the sample schools

Area	Status of Schools		Type of Schools		Strength of teachers (percentage)			Teachers strenth in School (No.)	
	Primary	Middle	Privateaided	Panchayat	Male	Female	Total	Adequate	inadequate
Trichuly	54	6	21	39	168	279	447	32	28
Aruppuk kottai	51	9	27	33	113	168	281	51	9
Total	105	15	48	72	281 (2.34)	447 (3.73)	728 (6.07)	83	37

Note: Figures with in parenthesis denotes the average number of teachers in a school.

2. Details of the sample schools

The survey was conducted in 120 schools in Trichuly and Aruppukkottai blocks. Of the 120 schools, 105 are primary schools and 15 are middle schools. The sample covers 48 private aided schools and 72 panchayat union schools. The average number of teachers employed in a school are 2.34 male and 3.73 female teachers. The strength of the teachers are also inadequate in more than 30 percent of the sample schools. These figures are given in Table - 5.

3. School Enrolment and Total Literacy Campaign

Tables -6 and 7 analysed the school enrolment in I standard and total strength of students in I to V standards during the period 1990-91 to 1993-94. It is clear that the average school enrolment in I Standard has decreased from 91.27 in 1990-91 to 78.6 in 1993-94. The total strength of the students has also decreased at an average from 401 in 1990-91 to 348 in 1993-94. It is also inferred that even though the TLC completed the first phase in this study district, the rate of school enrolment did not increase in primary schools.

4. Opinion of Head Masters on School Enrolment and TLC

The opinion of the respondents on the school enrolment are presented in Table-8. More than 60 percent of the respondents revealed that the school enrolment and strength could be increased by effective survey of teachers for identification and incentives like free uniform, Noon-meal scheme, scholarship etc.,

Child labour and poverty are the main causes for the poor strength in these schools of Kamarajar District. More than 65 per cent head masters accepted that the child labour in match industry and low income of the agricultural labourers reduced the students'strength.

The spread of population education in some village has created the problem of non availability of eligible age children for the schools. The small family norm and attachement of the parents with the town schools had affected the school enrolment in panchayat union schools in rural areas.

Table - 6
Details of school enrolment in I Standard of the sample schools (No.of Students)

Period	Trichuly			Aruppukkottai			Total		
	Male	Female	Total (percentage)	Male	Female	Total (percentage	Male	Female	Total (percentage)
Before TLC (1990-91)	1277	1058	2335 (38.92)	1734	1398	3147 (52.35)	3020	2456	5276 (91.27)
During TLC (1991-92)	1346	1027	2373 (39.55)	1647	1263	2910 (48.5)	2993	2290	5283 (88.05)
1993-94 1166	1003	2169	1373 (36.15)	1173	2547	1540 (42.45)	2176	4716	(78.60)

Note : Figures within the parenthesis denotes the average school enrolment in I Standard in a school.

TABLE - 7

Students strength in primary schools Before and After Implementation of TLC.

Period	Trichuly			Aruppukkottai			Total		
	Male	Female	Total (percentage)	Male	Female	Total (percentage)	Male	Female	Total (percentage)
Before TLC (1990-91)	5119	4296	9415 (156.92)	8052	6567	14619 (243.65)	13171	10863	24034 (400.57)
During TLC (1991-92)	4843	4222	9065 (151.08)	7746	6081	13827 (230.45)	12589	10303	22892 (381.55)
After TLC	5062	2606	7668 (127.80)	6963	5526	12489 (208.15)	12025	8132	20157 (335.95)
1993-94	4944	3955	8899 (148.32)	6507	5487	11994 (199.90)	11451	9442	20893 (348.22)

Note: Figures within the parenthesis denotes the average school strength of students.

5. Infulence of TLC on school enrolment

The influence of the TLC on school enrolment in study districts are exhibited in Table - 9. Only 16.67 percent of sample respondents accepted the influence of TLC on school enrolment through the motivation to parents and creating public awareness about the importance of literacy.

TABLE - 8
Opinion of respondents of School Enrolment

Sl. No. Opinion	No. of respondents viewed			
	Tri-chuly	Aruppu-kkottai	Total	Percentage
Enrolment increases				
Due to :				
i) Effective survey by teachers	16	21	37	30.83
ii) Compulsion of teachers	12	9	2'	17.50
iii) Incentives	23	17	40	33.33
iv) Motivation through TLC for parents	6	5	11	9.17
v) Public awareness about Literacy through TLC	3	6	9	7.50
vi) Others	-	2	2	1.67
Enrolment decreases Due to:				
i) Poor facilities in Schools	8	9	17	14.17
ii) Drought and poverty	21	20	41	34.16
iii) Child labour	23	17	40	33.33
iv) Shortage of teachers	2	3	5	4.17
v) Non-availability of eligible age students in villages	6	9	15	12.50
vi) Others	-	2	2	1.67

TABLE - 9
Influence of TLC on School enrolement

Sl. No.	Particulars	Tri-chuly	Aruppu-akkottai	Total
1.	Number of respondents accepted the influence of TLC on school enrolment	9	11	20 (16.67)
2.	Nature of influence			
	a. Motivation of parents	6	5	11 (9.17)
	b. Public awareness about literacy	3	6	9 (7.5)

Note: Figures with parenthesis denotes percentages to the total respondents.

The rest of 83.33 per cent of the sample respondents pointed out that since TLC developed the learning and writing practice for illiterate age group of 15-35 years, the school enrolment after TLC has not increased to the expected level. The school head masters suggested the following measures for increasing school enrolment through TLC:

i) TLC volunteers and school teachers may jointly conduct the door to door canvass campaign for enroling the children in schools.
ii) In collaboration with parent teacher's association, youth club, women's association etc., PLC may take steps to reduce child labour and effective implementation of poverty eradication programmes in villages; and
iii) TLC/PLC approach must be modified for the motivation of parents for their children's education.

6. Drop-outs from primary Schools

The Tamil Nadu average dropouts rate in 1993-94 was 20.32. The rate of dropout students from schools in I to V standard in Aruppukkottai division during the period from 1990-91 to 1993-94 are analysed in Tables - 10 & 11. It is clear that of the 120 sample schools, the number of schools having drop-out students increased from 91 in 1990-91 to 73 schools in 1993-94. Similarly the average dropout rate of students also decreased from 32.04 student per school in 1990-91 to 16.41 students in 1993-94. It is inferred that the average dropout rate of students per school has gradually decreased during the TLC (29.78) and after (28.2) and a sudden decrease in the year

TABLE - 10
Drop-outs from primary and middle schools in study districts

Year	Aruppukkottai						Trichuly						
	Standard						Standard						
	I	II	III	IV	V	Total	I	II	III	IV	V	Total	G. Total
Before TLC 1990-91	418	409	295	523	476	2121	276	186	183	204	102	1051	3172
During TLC 1991-92	323	403	189	375	334	1524	283	201	238	245	219	1186	2710
After TLC 1992-93	354	342	276	462	345	1779	264	206	165	193	185	1013	2792
1993-94	153	195	153	264	927	927	58	58	41	45	69	271	1198

Source : Computed from primary data.

TABLE - 11

Drop-outs from I to V standards in primary and middle in Aruppukkottai Division

	Trichuly				Aruppukkottai				Total			
Period	Boys	Girls	Total percentage	No.of School having drop-out	Boys	Girls	Total percentage	No.of Schools having drop-out	Boys	Girls	Total percentage	No.of school having drop out
Before TLC 1990-91	547	540	1051 (21.90)	48	1119	1002	2121 (41.59)	51	1666	1506	3172 (32.04)	99
During TLC 1991-92	603	583	1186 (15.78)	46	876	648	1524 (33.87)	45	1479	1231	2710 (29.78)	91
After TLC 1992-93	535	478	1013 (21.10)	48	1014	765	1779 (34.88)	51	1549	1243	2792 (28.20)	99
1993-94	139	132	271 (7.97)	34	555	372	927 (23.77)	39	694	504	1198 (16.41)	73

1993-94 (16.4) due to the various reasons. The reasons for the reduction in the dropout rate are discussed below:

The opinion of the respondents about the reasons for the dropout of students are exhibited in Table-12. The study found that the major reasons for the dropout of students are the problems of child labour (23.33 percent), poor facilities, lack of discipline in Panchayat schools and town atachement of parents to study in town/cities, (23.33 percent) and migration of agricultural workers, drought and poverty (20.83 percent) in this study district.

The TLC and PLC in this district tried to influence the students to continue the studies in schools. A large number of students participated in the TLC in this study district and they also created the awareness about literacy to the student friends.

In Kamarajar TLC District during teaching phase from October 1991 to June 1992, nearly 14,900 centres were opened in the villages and in the municipality wards to give practice to the learners in reading and writing and awareness. The district has achieved in imparting literacy to 1.53 lakhs learners and declared as'fully literate' district on October 10,1992.

TABLE - 12
Opinion of the respondents on the reasons for drop-outs

Sl. No.	Reasons	No of respondents viewed			
	Tri-	Arippu-chuly	Total kkottai	Percent-	age
1.	Match factory and child labour	8	20	28	23.33
2.	Poverty, drought and migration	17	8	25	20.83
3.	Poor facilities, discipline in village school and atachement of parents	11	17	28	23.33
4.	Child sibling and family problem	9	5	14	11.67
5.	Ignorance and illilitacy of parents	2	3	5	4.17
6.	Girl child help to parents	4	3	7	5.84
7.	Shortage of teachers	9	4	13	10.83

Source: Computed from primary data.

7. PARTICIPATION OF TEACHERS AND STUDENTS IN TLC

The participation of teachers and students from the sample study schools in this district are given in Table-13, Of the 120 sample respondents 31 participated in TLC as resource persons and co-ordinators. In Trichuly and Aruppukkottai study schools, 689 students were involved in TLC. The average number of students of a study school participated in TLC was 5.74. These figures show that large number of teachers and students has participated in TLC of Kamarajar District.

TABLE - 13
Participation of teachers and students in Kamarajar District TLC

Area	No.of teachers participated	No.of students participated			
		Boys	Girls	Total	Average
Trichuly	14 (23.33)	132	116	248	4.13
Aruppukkottai	17 (28.33)	276	165	441	7.35
Total	31 (25.83)	408 (3.56)	281 (2.98)	686 (3.30)	5.74

Note: Figures with parentheses denotes percentage

Table - 14 shows that the opinion of 44.17 per cent of the school head masters is that TLC eradicated illiteracy and provided writing and learning practice for the age group of 15-35 people. The opinion regarding the school enrolment of 15.83 percent respondents is that TLC motivated the students and parents for school enrollment and 19.16 percent accepted that TLC created awareness about the importance of literacy. From these results, it is clear that the view of the sample respondents that the TLC had played a major role in the eradication of illiteracy rather than for the awareness about literacy and motivation to parents.

TABLE - 14

Opinion of the respondents about TLC on School enrolment and drop-out

Sl. No.	Reasons	No of respondents viewed			
		Tri-chuly	Arippu-kkottai	Total	Percent-age
1.	TLC created awareness about the importance of literacy	12	11	23	19.16
2.	TLC motivated the students and parents for school enrolment	9	10	19	15.83
3.	TLC tried to eradicate illiteracy	12	8	20	16.67
4.	TLC eradicated illiteracy for the age group 15-35	24	29	53	44.17
5.	TLC did not bring any change in our village	3	2	5	4.17

Source: Computed from primary data.

SUMMARY AND CONCLUSION

In order to analyse the impact of TLC on school enrolment and drop-outs from primary schools in Kamarajar District, the study was conducted in two economically developed blocks-Trichuly and Aruppukkottai. The primary data were collected from 120 school head masters through interview method. The findings of the study are summarised below:

i) In Aruppukkottai educational division, more than 80 percent of the primary schools are panchayat union schools and the domination of private aided schools are comparatively low in this division.

ii) Girls enrolment (48.7 percent) in primary school of this division is higher than the national average of girls enrolment (45.7 percent).

iii) The strength of students is very low in panchayat union schools compared to private aided schools due to the poor facilities, discipline in panchayat union schools.

iv) The general characteristics of the sample respondents are (a) 56.67 percent of the headmasters are above 50 years of age; (b) 29.17 percent of respondents are female teachers working in primary schools;(c) More than 65 percent of the headmasters had completed the educational standard of SSLC; and v) Only 7.5 percent respondents belong to SC Community.

v) Of the 120 sample schools, 105 are primary and 15 are middle schools, The sample covers 48 private aided and 72 panchayat union Schools.

vi) The strength of teachers are inadequate in more than 30 percent of the sample schools.

vii) The study shows that after implementation of TLC in Kamarajar District, there was no increase in primary school enrolment. The average enrolment in I standard was decreased from 91.27 in 1990-91 to 78.6 in 1993-94. The total strength of students was also decreased, at an average per school, from 401 in 1990-91 to 348 in 1993-94.

viii) The opinion of the respondents is that the average enrolment and strength of students could be raised by the effective survey of teachers for identification. The respondents suggested for joint efforts of TLC with school teachers for motivation and effective survey at the time of school reopening period.

ix) Only 16.67 percent of headmasters had accepted the influence of TLC through motivation of parents, for increasing school enrolment in primary school.

x) After implementation of TLC, the number of schools having drop-outs students and the rate of students dropout from schools decreased from 32.04 students at an average per school in 1990-91 to 16.41 students in 1993-94.

xi) According to the opinion of sample respondents, the major reason for the dropouts from primary schools in the study district are the problem of child labour, attachment of parents, with town schools, migration of agricultural labourers and poor facilities in panchayat schools.

xii) A large portion of primary school headmasters (25.83 percent) and 3.3 percent of primary school students and participated in Kamarajar District TLC.

xiii) The study found TLC eradicated illiteracy and providing reading and writing practice particularly for the age group of 15-35 illiterate people. Only 15.83 per cent of teachers accepted the creating public awareness about literacy by TLC in the study district.

The motivation and awareness creating activities of TLC were not enough for raising the school enrolment in study district. After the successful implementation of TLC, the post Literacy Campaign could give much importance and modified approach for motivation to parents and awareness about the literacy.

4

READING MATERIALS TO THE NEO - LITERATES UNDER POST LITERACY CAMPAIGN

INTRODUCTION

Education is a liberating force only when it is available to all. "A Nation cannot survive being half free and half slave" declared Abraham Lincoln. It is an undeniable fact that our country faces two basic problems - poverty and illiteracy. Poverty immerses chunk of the population under economic dearth and deprivation. Illiteracy on its part combats, putting impediments on the path of development: Poverty and illiteracy combinely constitute the two faces for the miserable living of millions in India.

Human resources have been regarded as an essential part of all development work and planning, from this point of view, education is no doubt a capital input. Programmes have been formulated to "remove poverty" and to raise the mass above poverty line without removing illiteracy and ignorance as part would be futile. 1991 census has returned over 3,40,30,000 as illiterates in India. "A majority in India thus remain dark being kept away from the light of education".

About fifty percent of the illiterates belong to the most productive age group 15-35. This largely accounts for the snail pace of our qualitative economic development. Swami Vivekananda's words spoken about a century ago, are relevant even today:

> *"The only service to be done for our*
> *lower classes is to give them education,*
> *to develop their lost individuality.*
> *They are to be given ideas: their eyes*
> *are to be opened to what is going*
> *on in the World around them, and them they will work*
> *out their own salvations.*
> *Give them ideas; that is the only*
> *help they require and then the rest*
> *must follow as the effect".*

Mahatma Gandhi has rightly quoted that "Illiteracy is India's shame and sin and it must be wiped out".

The illiterates lack awareness and action. They suffer from poverty, disease and ignorance. A feeling of complete isolation is overcasting them subjecting them to political and economic deprivation. The educational system hitherto has been kept aloof from production. Job oriented or production oriented education has been neglected. It has neither provided skilled farmers to the villages nor developed a sense of respect for work, resulting in the shattering of the rural economic development. Until now our institutional education has failed to produce citizens who could successfully embody the national ideals such as "Secularism", "Socialism" and "Solidarity" who could combat anti-national activities like communalism, regionalism and linguism. Institution education expects the comforts of service oriented life with the ideals of promoting education with the above mentioned virtues while living in the society. The government has launched many schemes of which TLC and PLC form a vital component. These schemes try to remove the short comings of the institutionalised education with a pragmatic approach to imbibe these virtues along with their learning.

The post literacy campaign which is a continuation of the TLC was launched with the main objective of "Integrating the learning process to retain, improve and apply their basic knowledge, attitude and skill for the satisfaction of basic needs to permit them to continue education through a self-directed process for the improvement of their quality of life (personal and societal)".

The PLC was launched with the main intention of facilitating a continuous approach for after becoming literate, an adult generally becomes motivated to learn more things and shows more interest in reading different types of books and other published materials. He/she wants to use and develop his reading, writing skills. In general he wants to learn more and continues the process of education. It was felt that if suitable learning opportunities are not provided the neo-literates may lapse back to illiteracy. Keeping in view the need and importance of the extending educational opportunities to the neo-literates, the post literacy programme was launched.

The major objective of the post literacy is to reinforce and consolidate the skills relating to literacy among the learners, and to equip the learners with better knowledge, perception, skills, attitude, understanding, awareness, functionality etc., of the surrounding society and the nation at large. So they are equipped to remove the impediments coming in the way of leading a better, happier and more meaningful life that they become active members of the community and participate in the process of social reconstruction and national development. Thus in essence:

"The post literacy programme is being organised to reinforce and consolidate literacy skills of the learners on one hand and on the other, this will be the period when the learners with their better perception and critical understanding of the environment would be better equipped to remove the impediments coming on their way, they would be now more receptive to different economic programmes of the government and non-government agencies, grasping them and utilising them effectively, and the new awareness should facilitate them for the group action, including organisation of cooperative societies".

Thus in the light of the above background the objectives of the post literacy campaign could be broadly catogorised into;

1. To provide facilities to the neo-literates for stabilisation, reinforcement and upgradation of learning acquired by TLC.

2. To expand the services to those illiterates who are not covered by TLC.
3. To enable the semi-literates to achieve literacy levels as per the NLM norms.
4. Imparting purposeful and job oriented education and education that bridges the gap between learning and living so that the learners is well equipped in his or her own profession.
5. To disseminate information of the various developmental agencies involved in welfare programmes and obtain the assistance of various functionaries of the developmental agencies involved in welfare programmes and obtain the assistance of various functionaries of the developmental agencies at the centres, in order to impart vocational training in trades which can be of benefit to the community.
6. To motivate parents to send all their children to schocl with the main intention of reducing the school drop-out rate.
7. To create a forum for discussion and dissemination of information on immunisation, family welfare, social forestry etc.
8. To organise cultural and recreational activities for the benefit of neo-literates.
9. To organise environmental building activities to make people realise the need for education.
10. To coordinate the activities of non- formal education programme to cover 9-14 age group.

These objectives were formulated with the main intention of retention, continuation, reinforcement and application of literacy for development of the individual and the community. Thus, with this in purview the State Resource Centre was created for the implementation of the programme.

The State Resource Centre is the academic wing of the Directorate of Adult Education. The following are the main roles of SRC in the field of education:

- Curriculum development and preparation of teaching/ learning materials - publication of methodological guidelines as well as proto types.

- Training of Project Officers and Supervisors as well as of Resource persons who would assist the District Resource Units - also publication of training handbooks and other aids.
- Post literacy and follow - up materials - including review of existing literature, publication of new materials, issue of organisation guidelines.
- To organise seminars and symposiums to put across the objectives and activities of National Adult Education Programme.
- Assistance in environment building through mass media, publication of posters and other materials, exhibitions etc.
- Publication of books on adult and non-formal education, bulletines and periodicals in regional languages.

The State Resource Centre provides practically all the resource services to get the programme started. With the main zeal of producing innovative need based materials the centre adapts the following strategies in preparing materials for the neo-literates.

- Producing reading materials confirming to the needs of widely heterogenous age group of neo-literates.
- Preparation of sharpended and refined materials suitable to elementary reading and writing skills of neo-literates.
- Selection of suitable topics, content, language, illustration etc., which would arouse interest in a learner to read a book.

These issues require an intimate and objective understanding of the background and the environment of the neo-literates.

On the basis of an assessment of the needs of the learners and keeping in view the guidelines provided by the state government, the SRC has developed curriculum with teaching/learning materials prepared or adopted to suit the needs of the learners. The State Resource Centre has also conducted many researches and evaluation to monitor the effectiveness of the materials including formative evaluations of the materials.

With the main intention of analysing the relationship between the needs of the neo- literates and the materials supplied by the SRC has ventured into the task of conducting a research to study their needs. This research would enable the centre involved in the noble task of promoting literacy to print materials in accordance to the neo-literates needs, so that they are benefited to the core.

The present study attempts to analyse the impact of reading materials supplied under PLC to neo-literates in Madurai District of Tamil Nadu, which has been selected as the area of study.

Objective of the study

The specific objectives of the study are

1. To assess the needs and interest of the neo-literates in reading the post literacy materials in Madurai district.
2. To assess the supply of various reading materials to the neo-literates under PLC in Madurai District;
3. To find out the relation between the needs and the materials supplied to the neo-literates; and
4. To study the utility of broad sheet/newspaper/monthly/weekly magazine and books under PLC in Madurai District.

Research Methodology

The *modus operandi* of the research study is as follows:

This study is a descriptive analytical empirical study of the resource materials supplied to the neo-literates. The study was restricted to Usilampati division only among the 4 divisions of Madurai district. Usilampatti division covers six Panchayat unions, namely Usilampatti, Sedapatti, T.Kallupatti, Kallikudi, Thirumangalam and Sellampatti.

Of the 6 panchayat unions, 3 unions were selected for the study on the criteria that the blocks having highest number of PLC centres in the Usilampatti division would be selected. Form the selected 3 blocks, 9 panchayats were selected in the proportion of 3 Panchayats in each block. Of the 9 sampled panchayats, 135 neo-literates (15 neo - literates from each panchayat) were also randomly selected for the interview purpose. The respondents were interviewed with a Pretested Questionnaire.

Tools for data collections

A pretested questionnaire was used to interview the respondents. The questionnaire is catogorised into 5 sections. Section A deals with general particulars. Section B on the activities of the circle, Section C on the learners interests needs and opinions on the home journals, books, monthly Magazine subscribed to the centres.

Method of data collection

The method of interview adapted was" Direct/Guided in depth interview".

The study covers the PLC period of Madurai district from May 1993 to December 1994 secondary data and other relevant materials on post literacy campaign were collected from the District Arivoli Iyakkam office, Madurai. The study was conducted for a period of two months from October,94 - December'94.

Literacy campaign in Madurai district

The illiterates under the age group (15-35) in Tamil Nadu accounts for 5.8 millions. Total literacy campaign and post literacy campaign projects recently cover 7.45 million illiterates. This includes learners above 35 years also. The campaigns have been implemented in 21 districts. Of the 21 districts postliteracy campaign was completed in Kanyakumari, Kamarajar, Pududottai and Pasumpan districts. Post literacy campaign is in the process of being implemented in 10 districts namely Madurai, North Arcot, Ramanathapuram, Tirunelveli, Dindigul Anna and Coimbatore districts of Tamil Nadu.

The achievement of Madurai district in the Total literacy ohase is 76.38 percent against the total target of 3.28 lakh. Nearly 3.07 lakh learners have been enrolled. Among them 2.50 lakh learners have completed the level III.

The target age group for the campaign is (15-35) as per the sanction by the Ministry. In Madurai, post literacy project was sanctioned in May 1993 to cover 1.80 lakh neo-literates. As much as 1.35 lakh neo-literates are reportedly enrolled. About 1.08 lakh learners attended PLC as on May 1994. The approved cost for post literacy campaign is Rs.1.46 crores of which Rs. 0.97 crores was sanctioned from National Literacy Mission and Rs. 0.49 crores from the state government.

In Madurai district, each Panchayat union has one Block project Coordinator (BPC), 2 Assistant Project Coordinators (APC) and one Office Assistant for the implementation of PLC at block level. There is a library in each Panchayat maintained by the Panchayat Coordinator. The Panchayat Coordinator also coordinates and supervises the centres (vattam) in the Panchayat area. Generally each panchayat covers three to four centres which is guided by the Vatta Vazhikatti (Circle guide). Based on these administrative and organisational background, the vattam functions twice a week.

The following chart gives the organisational structure in Madurai District:

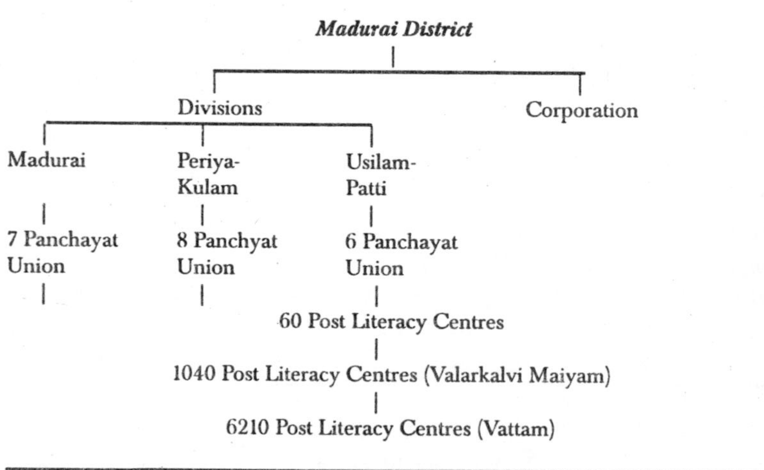

II. SOCIO - ECONOMIC PROFILE OF THE SAMPLE RESPONDENTS

The present section presents the demographic profile of the sampled respondents.

Age Group

Regarding the age group of the sampled spectrum, nearly 80 percent belonged in the age group (15-35), 1.3 percent were below the age group of 15 years and 9.63 percent were above the age group of 35 years.

TABLE-1
Age Group Pattern

Sl. No.	Panchayat	Age group			
		Below 15 yrs.	15-35 yrs.	Above 35 yrs.	Total
1.	T. Kallupatti	6	37	2	45
2.	Kallikudi	7	35	3	45
3.	Thirumangalam	1	36	8	45
	Total	14	108	13	135
	Percentage	10.3	80	9.63	100

Source: Computed from primary data.

Sex wise Distribution

Most of the respondents surveyed were females. Hence a safe inference could be drawn that the female respondents were much inspired by the Post Literacy Campaign. This shows that females were motivated much by the Post Literacy Campaign than males.

TABLE -2
Sex Wise Distribution

S.No	Panchayat	Male	Female	Total
1.	T. Kallupatti	11	34	45
2.	Kallikudi	13	32	45
3.	Thirumangalam	7	38	45
	Total	31	104	135
	Percentage	22.96	77.04	100

Source : Computed from primary data.

Caste Wise distribution

Of the total sample respondents, most of the respondents belonged to the Backward Class category (71 respondents), followed by SC/ST category (30.37 percent) and only a negligible 2.22 percent constituted the forward caste.

TABLE-3
Caste Wise Distribution

S.No	Panchayat	Community				
		B.C	M.B.C	SC/ST	FC	Total
1.	T. Kallupatti	25	-	20	-	45
2.	Kallukudi	18	10	15	2	45
3.	Thirumangalam	28	10	6	1	45
	Total	71	20	41	3	135
Percentage		52.59	14.82	30.37	2.22	100

Source : Computed from primary data.

Educational Background

TABLE-4
Literacy Level Of The Sample Respondents

S.No	Panchayat	TLC Comple ted	Dro outs from TLC	School Drop-outs	NFE Comp-leted	TOTAL
1.	T. Kallupatti	30	4	7	4	45
2.	Kallikudi	25	2	14	4	45
3.	Thirumangalam	19	4	21	1	45
	Total	74	10	42	9	135
	Percentage	54.81	7.41	31.11	6.67	100

Source : Computed from Primary Data.
Note : TLC refers to Total Literacy Campaign.

From the above table it could be infered that nearly 55 percent of the surveyed respondents have completed their Total Literacy Campaign. Nearly 7.41 of percent of the sample respondents enumerated as school dropouts and a negligible 6.67 percent had completed the Non-formal Education.

Economic Status of the Sample Respondents

TABLE-5
Occupational Pattern

S.No	Panchayat	Occupation				
		Agri-culture	Coolie	Busi-ness	Unempl-oyed	Total
1.	T. Kallupatti	8	33	2	2	45
2.	Kallikudi	10	25	3	7	45
3.	Thirumangalam	15	26	3	1	45
	Total	33	84	8	10	135

Source : computed from primary Data.

The study found that, 62.22 percent of sample respondents were collie labourers. Nearly 24.44 percent were agricultural labourers; 7.48 percent were unemployed and 5.93 percent were businessmen. Analysis of the family's annual income indicated 59.26 percent had annual income above Rs.6,400/- and 40.75 percent had below Rs.6,400/- per annum. This clearly reflects the prevailing poverty among the neo-literates. It is heartening that poverty has not dampened the spirit of these neo-literates.

TABLE-6
Annual Income Level of The Sampled Spectrum

S.No	Panchayat	Below	Above	Total
1.	T. Kallupatti	18	27	45
2.	Kallikudi	26	19	45
3.	Thirumangalam	11	34	45
	Total	55	80	135
	Percentage	40.74	59.26	100

Source: Computed from Primary Data.

* Hence from the socio-economic analysis of the sample spectrum, it could be safely deduced that most of the respondents belonged to the age group (15-35) which clearly elicits the fact that the materials published should suit the age group targeted.
* Secondly, it was found that most of the respondents were female. Hence, attention should be focussed on women issues. It is recommended that the curricula be more gender sensitive and offer materials relevant to their environment and interests.
* It is also suggested that the materials should be appropriately planned and focussed on developmental issues with special emphasis on the need of education for girl child stressing on the different socio-cultural reason for the non-enrollment of girl child in schools.
* The study also clearly illustrates the fact that nearly 40 percent of the surveyed respondents were below the poverty line. Hence, information of various developmental agencies involved in welfare programmes and welfare schemes available for their development should be disseminated through the materials.
* The materials should also incorporate messages necessary for day-to-day living like personal care, heath, child care, family welfare and other related issues.
* Since most of the respondents belonged to the category of coolie labourers and agricultural labourers, articles which evince significant knowledge on modern technology innovative strategies in the field of agriculture, legal information pertaining to wages and other significant issues could be highlighted.
* The survey also revealed that most of the respondents belonged to the backward, and SC/ST category. Hence, it would be appropriate to furnish details on reservations available for them in colleges/university and job preferences for SC/ST class.
* Since most of the surveyed respondents were in the age group of 15-35, more input could be given on technical education. Multi, skill training programme could be implemented to met rural job requirements. Information system on technology and linkages between the village problems and

science and technology could be incorporated as most of the respondents are in the employable age.

III. ANALYSIS OF THE MATERIALS SUPPLIED TO THE NEO-LITERATES

As part of its main work, the State Resource Centre undertakes evaluation research and resultant updating learning materials published by it.

This section presents an assessment of materials published by SRC and the short falls in the materials in meeting out the needs of the learners.

Venue for the functioning of the PL Centres

Research into this aspect revealed that 34 percent of the sample respondents attended classes at the houses of the circle guides. 24 percent attended classes at the neighbouring school campus; 27.4 percent at community centres and 14.08 percent under street lights. Survey threw light on deficiency in infrastructural facilities. Proper lighting facilities was found lacking in 7 percent community centres. School buildings had no lighting facilities at all.

TABLE-7
Veneue For The Functioning Of The Post-Literacy Centres

Sl. No.	Panchayat	Venue				
		School building	Street light	House of circle guides	Community centres	Total
1.	T. Kallupatti	20	4	11	10	45
2.	Kallikudi	9	12	12	12	45
3.	Thirumangalam	4	3	23	15	45
	Total	33	19	46	37	135
	Percentage	24.4	14.08	34.07	27.41	100

Source : Computed from primary data.

PARTICIPATION OF NEO-LITERATES:

The average number of neo-literates participated in a circle are presented in Table - 8.

TABLE-8

Average No. Of Neo-Literates Who Participated In The Circle Activities

Sl.	Patchayat	No. of neo-literates		Total
		Male	Female	
1.	T. Kallupatti	7	16	23
2.	Kallikudi	8	15	23
3.	Thirumangalam	10	19	29
	Total	25	50	75
	Average			25

Source :Computed from primary data.

The above table indicates that on an average, nearly 25 noe-literates attended the circles. Female respondents were inspired much by the Post-literacy Campaign.

Needs of the neo - literates and materials supplied under PLC

According to the National Literacy Mission, the materials prepared for the neo-literates should adopt a scientific procedure. Eminent educationists, subject specialists, language experts, research workers and experienced persons should be involved in the committee. Based upon proper evaluation results, the committee should recommend appropriate and adequate subject matter, written materials for the neo-literates.

The materials published should keep in view the local needs, language, dialect, culture etc. Efforts should also be made to produce appropriate follow-up materials, viz., books and other written materials, bulletins, news letters, periodicals, wall posters etc.

The 3 basic elements to be kept in view while planning a wroth while programme for post literacy are: a) Identification of learning needs of neo-literates; b) provisions of learning opportunities to meet the needs; c) Creating a socio-economic, political and cultural ambience to sustain the learning environment.

In this context it would be appropriate to focuss attention on poverty alleviation programmes, science and appropriate rural technologies to improve their quality of life after attaining literacy and after improving their awareness and their functional and vocational skills.

Awareness of laws, policies and programmes alone may not lead to achievement of the desired result. Post Literacy becomes a meaningful activity when it is preceded by systematic efforts for the formation of groups of neo-literates to come together. It should consolidate itself around worth while economic activities relevant to the lives of the neo-literates which would eventually result in conferring of ownership rights of assets to the members of the collective.

The National Policy on Education (NPE) 1986, resolved to implement post literacy and continuing education centres in rural areas. The programme of action elaborated the concept of continuing education as being essential for the 'learning society'.

The NLM aims at implementing the programme of post literacy by establishing libraries and reading rooms for public. It also envisages the introduction of latest technology in printing and publication of books, journals and newspapers.

The working group on national book policy states that local talent can be harnessed and local resources could be deployed for creating necessary motivation and producing initial library materials. The working group has recommended that the resources of the private book sector could be utilised for this purpose.

Distribution system of reading materials to the neo literates in Madurai District

Under Post literacy campaign, in Madurai district, Arivoli Continuing Education Centres or Arivoli Valar Kalvi Maiyams

(AVKMs) are established in each panchayat which covers two to four vattams or literacy circles. The distribution pattern of the reading materials are given in the flow chart below:

DISTRIBUTION PATTERN OF READING MATERIAL

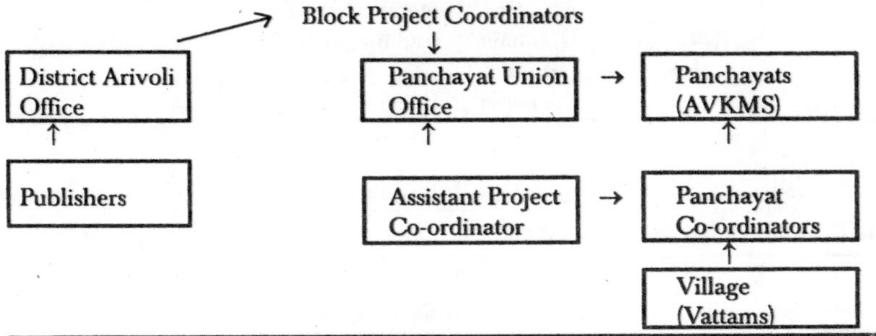

The State Resource Centre has prepared, designed and published curricula for the Non-formal/Adult Education Programmes. It has also prepared suitable teaching/learning materials, modules and software for these courses. These reading materials are supplied to the respective districts to be circulated to the neo-literates among the vattams. Some of the materials supplied to the neo-literates are newspapers, house journals like Yetram, Kudumba Malar etc.

This section presents in detail the opinion elicited by the neo-literates on the materials supplied to the centres in Madurai district.

IV. AN ASSESSMENT ON THE READING MATERIALS

A. Newspaper:

To keep the neo-literates abreast on current affairs of the country and world, newspapers are supplied to the centres. The Tamil daily 'Mallai Malar' earmarks a page for Arivoli news titled 'Arivoli Thendral'.

The 'Ariivoli Thendral' news is brought out by a team of experts covering a wide range of editions which includes stories on science and technology, weekly news round-up, literacy movement news and a section on readers contribution.

TABLE - 9

No. of Neo-Literates Who Have Read The Newspaper Mallai Malar With Arivoli Thendral

Sl. No.	Panchayat	No.of neo-literates who have not read the paper	No. of neo-literates who read the paper		Total
			Regularly	Rarely	
1.	T.Kallupatti	23	17	5	45
2.	Kallikudi	17	21	7	45
3.	Thirumangalam	11	22	12	45
	Total	51	60	24	135
	Percentage	37.78	44.44	17.78	100

Source: Computed from primary data.

From the above table it is clear that nearly 37 percent of respondents were not exposed to this newspaper. In this context analysis of factors inhibiting their motivation to make use of this information system was also made. Among 63 percent of the respondents who read paper 44.4 percent of the respondents read it regularly and 17.78 percent occasionaly.

On further analysis of the reasons for not availing the information service (newspaper) it was found that:

* Most of the learners were ignorant of the books specially written for them available with the centre.
* The number of copies subscribed were not sufficient.
* Most of the neo- literates has no time to read the paper

Hence, in this context the State Resource Centre and other agencies should examine the suitability of such books, even those brought out by private publishers and if possible, it should be brought to the notice of the learners while they are still in the centre.

If possible, these materials could be delivered at the homes of the learners on an experimental basis for at least one year. This may prove to be the cheapest and most effective follow-up programme.

Opinion of the neo-literates on "Malai Malar"

As regards to the opinion of learners on newspaper reading nearly 20.24 percent declared it useful, 82.14 percent interesting and 57.14 percent satisfying.

An analysis of the neo-literates favourite newspaper revealed the following facts:

TABLE - 10
Interesting newspapers of neo-literates

Sl. No.	Name of the newspapers	No. of neo-literates willing to read the newspaper			Total	Percentage
		T. kallupatti	Kallikudi	Thirumangalam		
1.	Daily Thanthi	14	15	9	38	28.15
2.	Dhina Malar	7	14	9	30	22.20
3.	Theekathir	4	5	13	22	16.29
4.	Dhinakaran	6	3	6	15	11.11
5.	Dhinamani	4	6	2	12	8.89
6.	Evening Papers	8	1	2	11	8.15
7.	Others	2	1	4	7	5.19
Total		45	45	45	135	100

Source : Computed from primary data.

The above table indicates that majority of the neo-literates read Daily Thanthi and Dhina Malar. In their opinion, language used in these papers is simple and easily understandable by the learners. This paper also covers stories, illustrations with pictorial representations which creates interest among the neo-literates. In addition, three books containing short stories, tit-bits and other interesting news are supplemented thrice a week with this paper. This paper was found popular among the respondents surveyed.

* It is suggested that popular papers like 'Daily Thanthi' and 'Dhina Malar' be supplied to the centres to disseminate information on current afairs, entertainment and other areas of interests.
* To promote a learning society, it is essential to supply reading materials appeasing the interest of the neo-literates. It could be rightly quoted that the aim of PLC should be to motivate the neo-literates.

  "To learn what he likes, at his own preferred pace, and from whosoever he likes, and to teach what he knows to those who desire to learnt from him".

Expectations of the neo-literates regarding articles published in the newspaper

When questions related to the neo-literates' interests and expectations about the articles published in the newspaper were posed the following recommendations emerged. The details have tabulated below:

TABLE - 11

Expectations Of Neo-Literates In Newspaper Supplied Under Post Literacy Campaign.

Sl. No.	Content in News paper	No.of neo-literates			Total	Percent-age
		T.Kallu-patti	kalli-kudi	Thiru-mangalam		
1.	Current Public News	22	12	31	65	48.15
2.	Cinema News	9	12	6	27	20.00
3.	Political News	5	6	4	15	11.11
4.	Short Stories	5	4	2	11	8.15
5.	Cultural Activities	3	6	-	9	6.66
6.	Other News	1	5	2	8	5.93
	Total	45	45	45	135	100

Source: Computed from primary data.

From the above table it is seen that (48.15 percent) were interested in news on current affairs, 20 percent on cine news. 11.11 percent evinced intrust in political and current affairs. Public news highlights information on the existing society, its value system, social, cultural, educational and political structures, divisions of power, the new society, that the nation desires to create; the role of individuals or social groups or institutions in creating the new society are issues with emphasis on the existing political scenario would be highly welcomed by the neo-literates.

* Cine news were their second choice of reading.
* It is suggested that the panel of experts involved in preparing the news articles give preference to the above mentioned facts. It is also suggested that certain messages can be spread using the celluloid fame artists and powerful tools.

B. Monthly and Weekly Magazines

Under the Post Literacy Campaign in Madurai district, two monthly magazines are subscribed namely 'Thulir' and 'Ariga Ariviyal'. 'Thulir' is a monthly magazine published by the Tamil Nadu Science Forum with financial assistance from the National Council for Science and Technology Communication and Department of Science and Technology, New Delhi.

"Ariga Ariviyal" is a monthly magazine focussing on scientific issues, published by Thavathiru Kundrakudi Adigalar in PMT District. Details of the neo-literates' exposure to these magazines are enlisted in Table - 12. From the table, it could be clearly inferred that only 12 percent of the respondents were exposed to these magazines and the remaining 88 percent have not read this magazines.

The reasons which inhibit their motivation is mainly due to the difficulty in understanding the scientific terms. The opinion study of these magazines have been exhibited in Table - 13.

TABLE - 12 :
Details Of The Monthly Magazine Readers

Sl. No.	Details	T. Kallupatti			Kallukudi			Tirumangalam			Total		
		T	AA	T & AA	T	AA	T& AA	T	AA	T & AA	T	AA	T & AA
1.	Number of neo-literates who have read the magazines	9	6	4	12	11	7	10	7	5	31 22.6%	24 17.76%	16 11.85%
2.	Number of neo-literates who have not yet received the magazine	36	39	4	33	34	38	35	38	40	104 77.4%	111 82.24%	119 88.15%
											135	135	135

Source : Computed from PRIMARY DATA
Abbreviations : T - Thulie, AA- Ariga Ariviyal

TABLE - 13
Opinion of The Neo-Literates About The Monthly Magazines

Sl. No.	opinion of neo-literates	Total No.of respon-dents	No.of neo-lite-rate who read magazines	Neo-lit-erate opinion No.	per-centage	Rank
1.	Difficult to under stand scientific terms	135	31	26	83.87	1
2.	Easy to read	135	31	19	61.29	2
3.	Creates changes in the approach of agriculture business and health	135	31	16	51.61	3
4.	Covers entertainment items	135	31	12	38.71	4
5.	Science news are not relevant to practical life	135	31	11	35.48	5
6.	Have no impact on readers	135	31	4	12.9	6
7.	Easy to understand scientific terms	135	31	5	16.13	7
8.	Book provides useful and interesting news on science	135	31	5	16.13	7

Source: Computed from primary data.

The list of the mothly /Weekly magazines of interest to neo-literates are presented in Table - 14.

TABLE - 14

Monthly/Weekly magazines of Interest to Neo-Literates.

Sl. No.	Name of the magazines	No. of neo-literates T. Kallu-patti	Kalli-kudi	Thiru-mangalam	Total	percentage
1.	Ananadavikadan	14	12	10	36	26.60
2.	Kumudham	7	6	7	20	14.81
3.	Kungumam	5	4	9	18	13.38
4.	Kalki	3	6	6	15	11.11
5.	Nakkeeran	6	3	3	12	8.89
6.	Rani, Devi	2	4	5	11	8.15
7.	Ariga Ariviyal	3	2	2	7	5.19
8.	Thulir	1	3	2	6	4.44
9.	Others	4	5	1	10	7.41
	Total	45	45	45	135	100.00

Source : Computed from primary data.

From the above table, it is clear that a majority of the neo-literates were interested in reading "Ananda Vikdan" (26.67 percent) followed by `Kumudam' (14.81 percent) and Kungumam(13.33 percent). Only a negligible few constituting 4.44 percent of the sample respondents were willing to read the monthly magazines, Thulir' and Ariga Ariviyal' (5.19 percent)

It is suggested that a copy of the weekly magazine 'Ananda Vikadan' may be subscribed to each Arivoli Valar Kalvi Maiyams.

Expectations of neo-literates in monthly/weekly magazines

With the main intention of incorporating the learners' needs and expectations in the house journals published by the resource centre, questions pertaining to the neo-literates expectations were posed. The results have been given in Table - 15.

Table-15:
Expected content in monthly/weekly magazines

Sl.No.	Expected contents by	Percentage
1.	Short Stories	28.89
2.	Cinema News	25.19
3.	Political News	20.00
4.	General Problems	17.78
5.	Science News	4.44
6.	Others	3.70

Source : Computed from primary data.

From the above table, it is seen that 28.89 percent were interested in short stories portraying educative and informative aspects. Cine news was their second choice of reading followed by political news.

C. Primers

Literacy not followed by the creation of meaningful reading materials is of little use. Due emphasis on the creation of meaningful reading materials is vital to attain the targeted goal.

Under the Post Literacy Campaign in Madurai District, the post literacy primers which are supplied include post literacy primer-I, Eatiki Potti and Yarukku Ethu Thevai.

Survey revealed that the three primers were interesting to the neo-literates and helpful in the retention of acquired skill of the participants. The primers were printed with required letter size suitable for neo-literates. The primers were presented in simple language with relevant interesting content. These primers are used by trained volunteers to teach the neo-literates at the respective Arivoli Vattam.

D. Books

The books material presented has to follow a certain pattern with regards to the size, cover, title, binding, page arrangements, print etc. Detailed planning on vital aspects such as (a) selection of the topic, (b) vocabulary used, (c) style of presenting the topic, (d) manner of presentation should be seriously considered.

In addition the reading material should be so devised as to be practicable for the teaching methods and those which arouse interest in a learner to read the book.

The Directorate of Adult Education, New Delhi has prepared a list of 1,200 titles for books to be used for neo-literates such that they encompass all aspects of human endeavour. On the basis of the size, cover, print and page arrangements these books are graded as I, II, III namely.

Grade-I 1-32 pages - 14 point type size
Grade-II 1-48 pages - 12 point type size
Grade-III 1-64 Pages - 12 point type size

Based on these topics, and grade the Madurai district post literacy campaign has published 61 titles of books. The details of the books supplied under Madurai District Post literacy campaign are presented in Table - 16.

Table - 16
Details of Books supplied under PLC in Madurai District

Sl. No.	Name of the Publishers	No.of books	Percentage	Total No. of copies supplied
1.	Madurai District Arivoli Iyakkam	6	9.48	14.000
2.	Tamil Nadu Science Forum Madras	8	13.11	3,500
3.	State Resource Centre for Non-formal Education, Madras	9	14.75	3,000
4.	Kalvi Gopalakrishnan	7	11.48	1,000
5.	Bharat Gyan Vigyan Samithi	10	16.39	2,500
6.	Kamarajar District Arivoli Iyakkam	21	34.43	8,500

Source: Computed from primary data.

From the above table, it is evident that they had purchased more than 90 of the books from other sources. The Madurai district Arivoli Iyakkam has published only 6 books which is not sufficient. In this context local resources and talents of the Key Resource Persons have to be fully utilised for the publication of books.

The 61 books used for the neo-literates could be catogorised into 6 main headings such as Health and Environment, Vocational Development and Employment, National Integration, Entertainment, Legal and General Awareness.

The study on the interest of the neo-literates on the 61 books supplied revealed that of the 61 books supplied by the PLC, 21 books were interesting and found useful to the neo literates which include 10 books on health and environment, 4 on vocational development and employment, 2 books on national integration and 1 on legal awareness.

The titles and the classification of the books considered to be useful and interesting are enlisted in Table - 17.

TABLE - 17
Useful and Interesting Books.

Sl.No.	Category and Title of books	No of Books
I.	*Entertainment*	4
1.	Kanbom Karpom	
2.	Nari Sonna Satchi	
3.	Vidukathai Podalama?	
4.	Anda panamum Paniyara Mazhayum	
II.	*Health and Environment*	10
1.	Neerinal Paravum Noigal	
2.	Saleyum Irumalum	
3.	Naam Yaen Noivai Padugirom?	
4.	Kamalavin Kavalai	
5.	Paen Thollaikku Sigitchai	
6.	Thel Kadikku Muthaluthavi	
7.	Sathunavu	
8.	Kudineerai Pathugappathu Yeppadi	
9.	Sugathara Kazhivu	
10.	Maramum Siruvanum	
III.	*Vocational Development and Employment*	4
1.	Arasu Nalathitta Uthavi Vazhikatti	
2.	Grama Kaithozhil	
3.	Vangi Thantha Vazhvu	
4.	Kalan Valarppu	
IV.	*Legal Awareness*	1
1.	Pengalum Sattamum	
V.	*National Integration*	2
1.	Neruvin Vazhvile	
2.	Suthanthira Poratta Thalaivargal	
	Tota	21

Source: Computed from primary data.

TABLE - 18
Books published under Madurai district PLC

S. No.	Title of The Books	Publisher	Price	Page	Message
1.	Barkalin Pathukappu	Kalvi Gopaila-krishnan Trust on behalf of Madurai Dist. Arivoli Iyakkam.	Free cost	20	To present the diseases of teeth
2.	Thee.. Thee.. Thee.. Thee...	- do -	- do -	20	Use of fire and other negative Industries
3.	Grama Kaithozhil	- do -	- do -	24	Self Employment and village Industries.
4.	Thel Kadikku Muthaluthavi	- do -	- do -	20	First aid for the bite by scoepion
5.	Pean Thollaikku Sigitchi	- do -	- do -	20	Preventive measures and reason for the growth of flies.
6.	Neruvin Vazhvile	- do -	- do -	28	Some events in the life of Nehru.
7.	Thavarathai	- do -	- do -	20	Importance of Green leaves and trees in forests.
8.	Sathu Mirantal	State Resource Centre For Non Formal Education S. Balasubramanian	Free cost	18	Women Problems - legal approach

{Cont.}......

9.	Kulanthai Nalam	R. Sivayanam Non-formal and Adult Edun. Iyakkam Madras - 6.	0.40	24	Maternal and Child Care
10.	Vangi Thantha Valvu	- do -	0.40	24	Savings and Self Employment.
11.	Viduthalai Poratta State Resource Thalaivaragal	Free cost centre for Non-formal Edun. MJA.Rajinadoss S.Balasubramanian	32		Life history about Thilak. Gokhale, V.O.C., Kumaran, Bose, Bagat Singh
12.	Kalan Valarppu	- do -	-do-		Methods of growth and uses of Mushroom in our life.
13.	Sathunavu	- do -	-do-		Healthy food items.
14.	Vidukathai Podalama	- do -	-do-		Collection of Jokes.
15.	Chiru Kudumbam Singara Thottam	SRC	-do-		Small Family Norms
16.	Chirithu Mazhaivom	- do -	-do-		Collection of Jokes
17.	Devathain Magal	Tamilnadu Science Form, Madras	Free cost	18	Short story
18.	Maramum Siruvanum	- do -	4.00	18	Benefits of Trees and Forests
19.	Tonic, Tonic	- do -	2.00	24	Child Care
20.	Panathin Kathai	- do -	1.00	18	Evolution of Money
21.	Yar Vallavar	- do -	2.00	24	Short Stories with Problems
22.	Maunin Madiyil	- do -	2.50	16	Natural Resources available in the earth.
23.	Pramavain Kathai	- do -	Free cost	24	Short stories
24.	Thannir...Thannir...	- do -	1:00	16	Importance of Water

{Cont.}...

25	Naam Yaen Noivai Padugorm?	Bharat Gyan Vigyan Samiti New Delhi.	free cost	20	Reasons for the spread of Diseases.
26.	Neerinal Paravum Neigal	- do -	free cost	24	Diseases due to the the water
27.	Kudineerai Pathugappathu	- do -	1.00	16	Drinking water without disease
28.	Sugathara Razhivirithu Selvam	- do -	2.00	24	Utility of Energy from Waste Products.
29.	Eitulum, Oliyum	- do -	2.00	16	Importance of Light or Sunshine
30.	Puthia Varugaikana Thayarippu	- do -	free cost	32	Preparation for the literacy neo-literates.
31.	Namal Mudivu Eattuka Mudium	- do -	- do -	16	Talent of neo-literates tested through problmes given as picture.
32.	Pen Arockiamum, Pen Urimaiyum	- do -	2.00	24	Women's Right and Health
33.	Annapathil ore Arputham	- do -	free cost	24	Short Stories
34.	Thaddupu Oosi	- do -	- do -	16	Importance of Preventive Measures Child Care and Maternal Care.
35.	Arasu Nalathitta Uthava Vazhikall	Madurai Dist. Arivoli Iyakkam	- do -	32	Awareness about the various Government Development Schemes
36.	Penkalum, Sathamum	- do -	- do -	20	Legal Protection to Women
37.	Eattiki Potti	- do -	- do -	20	Riddles
38.	Yarukku Eathu Devai?	- do -	- do -	16	Immediate need of some incident.
39.	Naam yan vaggamidukirom?	- do -	4.00	44	Functions of Arivoli Iyakkam etc.
40.	Arivoliyin suvaiyans	- do -	free cost	24	Interesting Events in

	Anupavangal				Arivoli Centres.
41.	Summava Sonarkal	Kamarajar Dist. Arivoli Iyyakkam Virudunagar	free cost	24	Collection of Short Stories
42.	Chella Kulanthai	- do -	- do -	20	Child Care
43.	Ulagam - Ammaukku Kaditham	- do -	- do -	16	About the World --1 Earth, Sun Nature etc.
44.	Ulagam - Ammaukku Kaditham - 2	- do -	- do -	16	- do -
45.	Neekkala Sollunkkal	- do -	- do -	24	Question and Answers from neo-literates.
46.	Thai	- do -	- do -	18	Age at Marriage and Maternal Care Activities
47.	Chali, Eurumal	- do -	- do -	24	Cough, Cold, Pneumonia Diarrhea Reason and Solution.
48.	Muthumalai Parisu	- do -	- do -	24	Question and Answers with Stories.
49.	Anta Panamum,	- do -	- do -	24	Short Story
50.	Siruthu Mazhilunkal	V. Rajaji, Madurai Dist. Arivoli Iyakkam	free cost	16	30 jokes
51.	Nari Chona Satchi	Kamarajar Dist. Arivoli Iyakkam	- do -	247	Short Stories by PLC Centre.
52.	Arivoli Vilaiyattukal	- do -	- do -	36	Playing methods at centre.
53.	Anju Rupa Puthagam-1	- do -	- do -	24	Folk Songs by PLC ' Learners-Collection,

{*Cont.*}....

No.	Title			Pages	Content
54.	Anju Rupa Puthagam -2	- do -	- do -	24	- do -
55.	Vaitru Poku	- do -	- do -	16	Disease of Diahorrea-Reason and Solution.
56.	Erumalum Saliyum	- do -	- do -	20	Reason for Cough and Cold and Preventive Measures,
57.	Kamalavin Kavalai	- do -	- do -	20	Disease through bad Waters Cholara and Typoid Disease.
58.	Akkayum Thangaiyum	- do -	- do -	20	Short Story helping to others without expecting any Return.
59.	Vidukathai Potalama	- do -	- do -	18	48 Riddles and Answers
60.	Kalamum, Naramum	- do -	- do -	24	Short Story
61.	Asao Kutuikathaigal	- do -	- do -	36	Collection of Short Stories.

Free cost refers to the cost of publishing the book born by the concerned District Arivoli Iyakkam and the book was distributed to the neo-literates at free price to motivate the learners to read the books. The minimum cost collected for some books in order to encourage the voluntary effort to read the books.

The rounded symbol 'o' denotes the interesting and useful books to the neo-illerates.

From the table 19 it is seen that 33% of the sample respondents were interested in vocational and employment oriented books. It is likely that acceptance or reading will be effective of an adult is started on a book dealing with his own craft. The newness of knowledge communicated in the books will induce the learners to persist in reading for the new knowledge could be immediately put to use to his economic advantage.

Books with cooking instructions and art wave designing exercise evinced significant interest among women learners, this is evident from the table 18. 52% of the respondents were interested in this issues.

Table - 19

Expectations of the neo-literates in the Post Literacy Campaign Books

Sl No.	Expectation of neo-literates	Neo-literates 1	2	3	Total	percentage
1.	Vocational development & employment	14	14	16	44	32.59
2.	Cooking instructions and designed art wave exercises (kolam) for women	12	11	2	25	18.52
3.	Historical short stories	8	4	9	21	15.56
4.	Legal Awareness	3	8	9	20	14.81
5.	Innovative agricultural & Science techniques	4	3	4	11	8.51
6.	News-Cine Songs	2	3	4	9	6.67
7.	Health	2	2	1	5	3.70
	Total	45	45	45	133	100.00

1 - T. Kallupatti 2 - Kallikudi 3 - Thirumangalam
Source: Computed from primary data.

Short stories depicting historical events were their third choice followed by cine songs and health issues.

* It is suggested that emphasis should be given on craft centred series of books like farming, spinning, carpentry, poultry

farming, animal husbandry, pottery, basket making, bee keeping, dairying, fishery etc.

* Books focussing on employment and vocational development would induce the neo-literates to persist in reading for the knowledge acquired could be immediately put to use to his economic advantage for "Economic aspects overpowers other factors in the promotion of interests in subjects for study".

Hence it is suggested that the panel of experts involved in preparing books for neo-literates give preference to the above mentioned facts.

V. CONCLUSION AND RECOMMENDATIONS

The present section briefly summarises the study as detailed in preceding section and then gives some important recommendations based on the field study.

General Background

a. **Age Group** : It was found that most of the respondents (80 percent) belonged to the age group 15 - 35.
b. **Sex-wise Distribution**: It was found that most of the neo-literates were female (77.04 percent)
c. **Caste-wise Distribution:** The schedule castes, backward castes and most backward castes constituted 90 percent among the surveyed respondents.
d. **Occupation:** An analysis of the occupational background revealed that majority of the respondents (62.22 percent) were coolie labourers.
e. **Educational Background:** It was found that most of the respondents had completed their literacy courses under the TLC phase.
f. **Annual Income**: Analysis of the income level indicated that 59.20 percent had annual income above Rs.6,500/- and the remaining less than Rs.6,500/-

ANALYSIS OF THE ACTIVITIES AND MATERIALS SUPPLIED UNDER PLC

a. Venue for the functioning of PL Centres

Research into this aspect revealed that 34 percent of the sample respondents attended classes at the house of circle guides. 24 percent attended classes at the neighbouring school campus. 27.74 percent at community centres and 14.08 percent under street lights.

b. No. of neo-literates who participate in the PLC

It was evident that on an average nearly 25 neo-literates attended the circles, among them, female respondents were inspired much by the PLC.

Needs of the neo-literates

This section highlights on the importance of publishing need based materials and the strategies to be adopted for the same.

1. Newspaper

a. Newspaper (Malai Malar)

Research indicated that 37 percent were not exposed to this news paper. Among 63 percent of the respondents who read paper 44.4 percent read it regularly and 17.7 percent occasionally.

b. Newspaper of interest to neo-literates

About 50 percent of the neo-literates read 'Dina Thanthi' and 'Dina Malar' and only 8.15 percent of them were interested in reading 'Malai Malar' which is circulated in the PL centres.

c. Expectations of the neo-literates regarding articles that could be published in the newspaper for neo-literates

It was analysed that majority of the respondents were interested in current public news, followed by political and cine news.

2. Monthly and Weekly Magazines

a. Exposure to 'Thulir' and 'Ariga Ariviyal'

Research indicated that only 12 percent of the respondents have read the magazine, remaining 88 percent have not yet read these magazine.

b. opinion on the Monthly magazine 'Thulir' and 'Ariga Ariviyal'

Among the 31 respondents who have read the magazines majority of the respondents opined that the scientific terms were difficult to understand.

c. Monthly/Weekly magazines of interest to neo-literates

Neo-literates prefer the magazine 'Aananda Vikatan', 'Kumudam' and 'Kunkumam'.

d. Expectations of the neo-literates on articles that could be incorporated in the home journals.

Majority of the respondents evinced interest in short stories, cine news and political news.

3. Primers

Survey revealed that majority of the respondents found the primers to be useful and interesting.

4. Books

a. Details of books that are circulated in the PLC

Survey revealed that only 6 books were published by the Madurai district Arivoli Iyakkam, and more than 90 percent of the books were purchased from other sources.

Of the 61 books circulated only 21 books evinced interest among the neo-literates.

b. Expectations of the neo-literates in the PLC books

Research directed in this aspect revealed that 33 percent of the sampled respondents were interested in vocational and employment oriented books.

Women neo-literates were interested in books containing cooking instructions and other related issues.

Neo - literates were also interested in books related to historical short stories, cine songs and other entertainment issues.

C. SUGGESTIONS

As stated earlier the above brief summaraisation of the contents of the research was one with a view to highlight same significant aspects related to the suggestions are implied in the summary itself, the following are some major recommendations on the basis of the study.

1. It is suggested that reading materials should emphasise in imparting literacy skills of persons belonging to the economically and socially deprived sections of the society.
2. The materials should be suited to the interest of adult and reading needs to achieve tangible progress. The literacy materials should draw its materials from the interests of the adults. For this purpose a small sample study of adult interests may be made by the concerned centres to provide "Need based literacy".
3. It is suggested that one additional library can be started in each districts as libraries by their very nature are centres for the spread of knowledge and information and as such they can play a vital role in the spread of literacy and the education of our masses. Hence, it is essential that all activities connected with adult education programmes are built around the libraries.

4. It is suggested that assistants should be employed in each panchayat to distribute the reading materials to the centres and to help the neo-literates to read the books on a rotation basis.
5. The department should recruit competent instructors and they should be given proper training. Possibilities of extending continuous training facilities should be explored.
6. The supply of news papers, home journals and monthly/ weekly magazines should be up-dated to keep the neo-literates abreast of current affiars.
7. More than two copies of books, magazines and news papers should be distributed to the centre to solve the problem of non-availability of reading materials.
8. In addition to the supply of reading materials, legal advisers rural development officers, primary health centre workers should be invited to the PLC centres and periodic interaction sessions should be held with the learners to clarify their doubts.
9. It is suggested that emphasis should be given on craft centred series of books like farming, spinning, carpentry poultry farming in reading for the knowledge acquired could be immediately put into practice. The content should cover the following aspects:
    a. Identifying the availability of raw materials in the locality.
    b. Feasibility of producing the identified products.
    c. Technical skills
    d. Marketing facilities.
10. The talents of the Key Resource Persons, Writers, Poets and Celluloid fame artists should be fully utilised to propagate the message of literacy with the main intention of "PROMOTING LEARNING SOCIETY".

5

POPULATION EDUCATION MESSAGE TO NEO LITERATES

INTRODUCTION

The global population was 3010 millions in 1960 and it has increased to 5380 millions in 1991. At the current rates, in 2000 year, the population is likely to touch 6220 millions i.e., it will double itself in four decades (1960-2000). According to 1991 census, India's population was 846 million and the UN World population report, 1994 shows that the population of India is 896.6 millions. According to UNDP's projections, it is likely to cross 1000 millions mark at the current growth rate by the end of the present century.

Population control strategies have been in the forefront of Indian planning for many decades now. The nature and dimensions of the population problem is such that unless it is linked to various developmental and educational programmes, its chances of success become minimal. It is absolutely imperative, therefore, that millions living in, as vast a country as ours, need to be educated about the implications of a population explosion. It is here that the role of the National Literacy Mission becomes increasingly important. At a time when literacy campaign is sweeping across the country, population education strategies deserve special importance.

Total Literacy Campaigns being implemented in, are creating awareness about the population issue also. Small family norm is one of the issues of national concern and forms and essential part of literacy material. State Resource Centres are preparing the variety of relevant and quality materials for environment building activities and imparting training. Under Post Literacy Campaign (PLC), supply of reading materials, health campaign, and discussion among the women neo-literates have enrich the awareness about the family welfare activities.

Evaluation of several literacy campaigns has indicated a very positive impact of these campaigns on the attitude of target population in realising and accepting the value of small family norm. The present study attempts to assess the knowledge, attitude and practice of neo-literates of Post Literacy Campaign about population issues in Ramanathapuram and Tirunelveli Kattabomman Districts of Tamil Nadu.

Objectives of the study:

The specific objectives of the present study are:

i. To study the socio-economic conditions of the neo-literates under post literacy campaign;
ii. To assess the level of understanding of the respondents about the advantages and disadvantages of early marriage.
iii. To measure their awareness of family planning methods, small family norms, maternal and child care activities;
iv. To study their attitudes towards family planning methods and the acceptance level; and
v. To find out the infant and child mortality level in the study population.

Methodology - Design of the study:

Ramanathapuram and Tirunelveli Kattabomman Districts were purposively selected for the Knowledge, Attitude and practice (K.A.P) study among neo-literates of Post Literacy Campaign. In these two districts, the Post Literacy Campaign was started in the year 1993 and during the study period, the campaign is in the final stage of completion. After selecting the districts, two sample blocks in each distri·t selected with the consultation of the Literacy Campaign Officials. Based on the criteria that the best performed blocks under

Total Literacy Campaign in the District, 4 Blocks were selected as sample Blocks, namely, Paramakudi and Kamuthi in Ramnathapuram District and Vasudevanallur and Keelapavoor in Tirunelveli Kattabomman District. The performance of the literacy campaign was already evaluated by the Madras Institute of Development Studies in Ramanathapuram District and by Karaikudi Alagappa University in Tirunelveli Kattabamman District.

After selecting the four sample Blocks in two districts, five villages in each Block were selected on the basis of the criteria that the village having the large number of active women neo-literates under PLC. The sample villages are Koonakulam, Ponnakarai, Vanthoni, Undothi and Parkankurichi in Paramakudi Block, Kilamaram, Perumaldevanpatti, Keelaramanathi, Ramasamypatti and Kattaimedu in Kamuthi Block, Viswanathapery, Thenmalai, A. Subramaniapuram, Meenakshipuram and Devipattnam in Vasudevanallur Block and Avudaiyanoor, Muthukrishnapery, Thayarthopper, pethanadarpatti and Adaikalapattnam in Keelapavoor Block. A total of 20 villages were selected with the discussion of Arivoli functionaries of the concerned blocks and districts.

The 15 sample PLC learners in the age group of 15-45 were randomly selected in each villages. Since the contraceptive practice is applicable only to the respondents in the reproductive age. Care was taken to select the sample respondents as married and in the determined age group. Thus, purposive random sampling method was used for identifying the sample respondents. A total of 300 respondents were interviewed with the pretested questionnaire.

Primary data were collected from the 300 sample respondents. The questionnaire was prepared in English consisting of the socio-economic profile, knowledge, attitude and practice of family planning methods, Maternal and child health, Age at Marriage and child Mortality. The data was collected during the period from the month of August to October 1995. The collected data were analysed by using the descriptive and percentage analysis. Secondary data relating to the PLC learners, census and heath indicators, District profile and related past studies were also collected from the concerned

Department of Family welfare, District Collectorate and from various Books, journals and research reports in the libraries.

Limitation of the study:

The main limitation of the study is that the survey was conducted only from PLC leaners who did not have any records and lack of memory regarding the age at marriage, pregnancy details, family planning messages etc. Care was taken to elucidate the accurate information from the respondents during the interview period.

II. REVIEW OF LITERATURE

This section reviews some important past studies relating to the Knowledge, Attitude and Practices on the family Welfare, health activities and population education issues.

Chandrsekar, (1972) in his book, revealed that perhaps the most difficult problem before low-income and technologically backward countries like India is the choice of a contraceptive that is acceptable under poor living conditions, particularly in the depressed rural areas where privacy, running water, electricity, any knowledge of reproductive physiology and most important, motivation, are more or less absent. Besides, in India's vast hetrogeneous population no single method, however good, can be suitable to all. Hence 'the cafeteria approach' that has been adopted in India.

Another study V.A. Pai Pannanlikar, Ajay K. Mehra, 1987) found that there is a need for a shift in the public policy towards a conscious mobilisation of the people for accepting family planning. Such mobilization cannot be achieved through the bureaucracy. Indeed participation and bureaucratization the lesser perhaps will be the people's participation. The mobilized participation has 'therefore' to be attained through non-bureaucratic institution and organisation.

Narayana Namboodiri (1972) conducted a study in Madurai District and found that practice of modern contraception is very negligible in all the caste groups. Abortion as a method of contraception is widely practiced by the higher caste. Economic status is positively associated with fertility in general with depression at the highest income category namely Rs.3000 or more per annum.

The study of Kivlin (1989) found that caste, education of both respondent and wife, level of living and literacy of the respondent were all positively and significantly related to knowledge, approval and adoption of vasectomy and the loop.

Mahadevan pillai (1972) found that raising age at marriage of girls and boys is not likely to meet with opposition. However, the lower socio-economic group may need some persuasion. There appears to be a need for introduction of population education in and outside schools particularly for girls.

The conclusions of the study(P.K Bhargava and P.C Sazena, 1985) revealed the role and importance of female education and work participation in economic activity in raising the age at marriage. In a country like India, where births occur primarily within the institution of marriage, an effective population policy incorporating well directed plans.

A study (C.K.Chacko, 1978) conducted in Ramanathapuram District and found that number of living children is found to be higher among adopters than non-adopters irrespective of religion. Hindus tend to adopt family planning methods comparatively at an early stage than Christians and Muslims. Tubectomy accounts for almost 100 of the methods adopted by the study population.

The study of Srivastava (1986) suggested that relatively larger emphasis is given to expansion of female education within the overall strategy of educational expansion. Female education is the main determinant of female status. Literacy status influence the male and female marriage ages.

Another study of Rajeswari (1987) found that 70 per cent of laparoscopic tubectomy acceptors were illiterate, 26.5 percent were educated upto middle school and below and 1.6 per cent were educated upto high school. The respective figures among conventional tubectomy acceptors were 68.6 per cent, 25.6 per cent and 4.1 per cent. The method requires no hospitalisation, so that, the acceptors easily accept this method.

The study (M.M. Gandotra, 1987) of various reasons for non-adoption of family planning revealed that significant proportion of such reasons has arisen due to the psychological fears and misconception associated with the use of scientific methods of contraception. In view of this, the role of extension education by the health staff can not be undermined.

An analysis of Rama Rao,(1985) in a study, found that the relationship between fertility and mortality, in general, infant and child mortality, in particular, has occupied a central place in demographic research. Notestein (1945) and Dany (1945) were of the opinion that mortality decline would lead to fertility reduction. Freedman (1961-62) while reviewing the literature on fertility, indicated that a secular decline in marotality must eventually produce a decline fertility. Freedman (1963) also argued that low mortality is all of the necessary condition for an effective social policy for reducing fertility.

A study by Ramachandra Sastry (1979) revealed that there are no significant differences in awareness of contraceptive methods but a higher percentage of non-adopters have negative attitude towards family planning methods. Women are more aware than men but higher percent of women have negative attitude towards family planning. The negative attitude of the females towards family planning methods perhaps due to the fact that the female sterlisation has scope for certain side - effects. Probably the dissatisfied acceptors are influencing their attitude.

Radha Devi (1979) conducted a study in Madurai District and found that vasectomy appeared more popular among the low socio-economic class. The desire to adopt any permanent conception control method is felt only after the attainment of exceeding the desired number of children, but actual adoption depends on the physical ability of the wife to produce children; knowledge and faith in the method to be adopted; achievement of desired sex ratio among children, and a favourable atmosphere at home and in the family for adoption of sterlisation.

Another study (K. Ramachandra Sastry, 1983) attempted to identify the factors that would explain the gap between awareness and adoption of contraceptive practices and found that while female and male sterilization is widely, known, awareness, among women, of temporary contraceptives is low. Condom and sterilization are reported more effective than IUD. Motivational campaigns should be specially directed to the young parents to encourage use of temporary methods for birth spacing.

A KAP study (Z.H. Qureshi and Samiur Rahman, 1993) of State Resource Centre, New Delhi revealed that due to literacy project activities in terms of overall knowledge scores, there was a 40 percent increase in 'high' knowledge category of the respondents. As a result of their exposure to the project's activities, the respondents were able to acquire knowledge on population issues which helped them in `appreciating' the problems of our population leading to the development of favorable attitudes. Use of public health and family welfare services for family planning counselling and service increased among the respondents. Majority of the respondents and their spouses were married at an early age. They had 3.2 children on an average, born at an interval of 29 months.

The earlier studies reviewed, so far, would help to understand the analyse of the present KAP study on the PLC learners with specific reference to population Education Message in Ramanathapuram and Nellai Kattabomman Districts of Tamil Nadu.

III. PROFILE OF THE STUDY DISTRICTS AND THE POST LITERACY CAMPAIGN.

The study was conducted in Ramnathapuram District and Nellai Kattabomman District of Tamil Nadu. The limited scope of the study is a specific reference of population education message to the learners of Post Literacy Campaign. It is imperative to analyse the socio-economic profile of the study districts and a brief profile of the post Literacy Campaign in the districts.

1. Profile of Ramnathapuram District and the Post Literacy Campaign:

Ramanathauram is a coastal area in the most backward among all the Districts of Tamil Nadu. It is surrounded by Pudukottai District on the North, Pasumpon Muthuramalingam and Kamarajar Districts on the North West and West, V.O. Chidambaranar District and Gulf on Mannar on the South and Palk strait on the East. The district has an area of 4216.41 square kilometres. The unique feature of the district is its longest coastal line measuring about 265 kilometres accounting for near by 1/4 of the total length of the coastal line of the State.

The climate is generally hot and dry and the district receives scanty rainfall only 1871.8 mm from the North East Mansoon. There are no perennial rivers in the district. Vaigai is the only major river which enters this district near Paramakudi and flows through Ramanathauram and falls in the Ramanathapuram big tank.

According to 1991 census, the District has a population of 1,135,887 which constitutes 562.387 males (49.5 percent) and 573,500 females (50.5 percent). The rural population (886195) constitutes 78 percent of the total population. The density of population per sq.km.is 268. The percentage of workers to total population is 46 and 2/3 of the workers derive employment from Agriculture only. About 10 percent of the active marine fisherman in Tamil Nadu are living in this district.

For administrative convenience, this District has been divided into two Revenue Divisions, namely, Ramnathapuram and Paramakudi, There are 6 taluks, 11 Panchayat Unions, 444 Panchayats, 2156 villages, 2 Municipalities and one township in this district.

Regarding the family welfare facilities, there are 9 Government Hospitals, 5 urban family welfare centres, 3 post martum centres, 5 taluk hospitals, 3 non-taluk hospitals, 11 Primary Health Centres, 2 upgrade Primary Health Centres, 255 sub-centres, 6 MTP approved Centres, 15 approved Private Nursing Homes in the district.

According to the 1991 census report, the vital rates are, 23.2 Birth rate, 7.7 Death rate, 64.8 Infant Mortality Rate, 1.6 Maternal Mortality Rate. The age at marriage is 23 for males and 19 females. The average

age of family planning acceptors are 32.7 for vasectomy (spouse) 28.9 for tubectomy and 26.2 for IUD. The table 1 revealed the target and achievement of family welfare programme during 1992-93, in the Ramanathapuram District. It is clear that during the period 1992-93, 20,619 percents had adopted the various family planning methods in the district.

Table - 1
Target and Achievement under Family Welfare Programme during 1992-93 in Ramanathapuram District

Sl.NO.	Method	Target	Achievement	Percentage
1.	Sterlisation	10,000	6595	65.9
2.	I.U.D	10,000	6555	65.9
3.	C.C.users	5,100	3432	67.3
4.	O.P users	6,700	4037	60.3
5.	Immunisation-DPT	10,21,300	11,03,034	108
6.	,, T.T (Mothers)	13,23,400	11,82,800	89

Source : Family Welfare Department, Ramnathapuram

The Total Literacy Campaign (TLC) in Ramanthapuram District was launched in the month of April 1992 and identified (9 to 45 age) 2 lakh illiterate persons comprising of 68,000 males and 1,32,000 females. An internal evaluation by Madras Institute of Development Studies revealed that more than 80 percent of the learners who had completed primmer III, had secured grading above 80 percent.

During the Post Literacy Campaign (PLC) the same target group of 2.00 lakh persons were considered as neo-literates. Learning Programmes like village library, wall newspapers, guest lectures, village cultural shows etc. are organised, The PLC are conducted over a period of two years starting from September' 93. The neo-literates of PLC in Ramnathapuam District formed a neo-literate organisation in the name of "Ramnathapuram District Women Development Organisation". This society is conducting meeting in every village, and propagating the idea of gender equity, empowerment of women, economic independence for the women folk in villages, education for girl children, women and child care, family planning, immunisation family hygiene etc.

2. Profile of Tirunelveli Kattabomman District and the post Literacy Campaign:

Tirunelveli Kattambomman District is located in the south eastern part of Tamil Nadu. But for Kanyakumari District, this is the southern most district bounded by Kamarajar district in the north, V.O. Chidambaranar district on the east, Gulf of Mannar and Kanyakumari district on the south and Western Ghats and Kanyakumari district on the west. The district extends over an area of 6,42,728 hectares accounting for 4.95 percent of the total area of Tamil Nadu.

The district comprises of 10 Taluks, 3 Revenue Divisions and 19 Panchayat Unions. The total population of the district is 24,93,189 as per census 1991. The density of population per square kilometre is 366. The population in the rural areas is 17,02,468 (68.28 percent) and that of the urban area is 7,90,721 (31.72 percent). The population consists of 12,24,319 male (49.11 percent) and 12,68,870 female (50.89 percent). Of the total workers, nearly 25 percent are cultivators while 29 percent are engaged as agricultural labourers. Thus, 54 percent of workers are engaged in agricultural sector.

The normal rainfall for the district is 814.8 mm compared with state normal rainfall of 1008.1 mm, it is low. The river Tambiraparani, rises from Agastiar Malai in Pothigai hills in the Western Ghats passes through Ambasamudram, Tirunelveli, Turicorin and Thiruchendur. The best irrigated lands in the district lie on either side of this river. The rest of lands are dry and undulating.

Regarding family welfare facilities, there are 8 Government Hospitals, 9 Urban Family Welfare Centres, 12 Health Posts, 6 Post Partum Centres, 4 Taluk Hospitals, 4 Non-Taluk Hospitals, 63 Primary Health Centres, 2 upgraded Primary Health centres, 385 Subcentres, 35 MTP Approved centres, 28 Approved Private Nursing Homes in the Tirunelveli Kattabomman districts.

The vital rates (1989-90) are as follows: Birth Rate-21, Death Rate 8.1, Infant Mortality Rate 59.0 and Maternal Mortality Rate 2.1. The age at marriage is 25.7 for males and 20.0 for females. The average age of acceptors are 31.8 for vasectomy (spouse), 28.1 for tubectomy and 25.9 for I.U.D. The target and achievements under family welfare programme in the district during 1992-93 are given in Table 2.

TABLE 2

Target and Achievement under Family Welfare Programme During 1992-93.

Sl.NO.	Method	Target	Achievement	Percentage
1.	Sterlisation	21,000	14,886	70.9
2.	I.U.D.	20.000	19.319	96.6
3.	C.C. Users	14,700	16.616	113.6
4.	O.P. Users	10,000	8,615	86.1
5.	Immunisation-T.T.mothers	57,200	56,244	98
6.	,, D.P.T.	44,500	48,085	108

Source: Family Welfare Department, Tirunelveli.

The table 2 revealed that 59,436 persons adopted the various family planning methods during a period of year 1992-93 in the Tirunelveli Kattabomman District.

The Total Literacy Campaign was started in the month of November, 1991. The identified illiterate (15-35 age) was 2,80,000 in the district. An evaluation study was conducted by the Centre for Adult, Continuing Education and Extension,

Alagappa University and found that 2,000,000 illiterates completed the Primer-I and 1,70,000 completed the Primer II in the Tirunelveli Kattabomman District.

The Post Literacy Campaign (PLC) was started on 15th April 1993 in the district with the same enrolment of TLC. Under PLC, health campaign, gender equity, science exhibitions awareness about development schemes and training for self employment were also conducted in the district.

Based on the above said socio-economic profile of the Ramnathapuram and Tirunelveli Kattabomman Districts and the implementation of the Post Literacy Campaign, the present KAP study was conducted on the PLC learners in these two districts with specific reference to the population education messages.

IV. RESULTS AND DISCUSSION

The primary data collected from the 320 sample respondents in two districts are analysed in this section. The section is divided into three sub-divisions. The first sub-division of analysis focus the socio-economic profile of the respondents. The Knowledge and Attitude of the respondents on the population issues are discussed in the second sub-division. The third sub-division describes the family welfare practices of the respondents in the study districts.

A. Socio-Economic Profile of the Respondents:

The findings of the study about the socio-economic conditions of the PLC learners in the study districts - Ramanathapuram and Tirunelveli Kattabomman districts, are presented as a descriptive analysis.

1. Age

The literacy campaigns (TLC and PLC) cater to the age group of 15 to 35 years which forms the most crucial part of reproductive life span i.e., 15-49 years. Therefore, an investment in this age group (15-35) in terms of population education may yield immediate results leading to fertility control. The age wise distribution of the respondents are given in Table 3.

The study showed that the majority of the sample learners (79.33 percent) are belonged to the age group of 18 to 45 years. This age group are favourable and suitable for the KAP study on the population education message through literacy campaign and useful for the fertility control measures. The study only covered the 18.67 percent of sample learners in the age group of above 45 years.

TABLE: 3
Agewise Distribution of the Respondents

Sl. No.	Study Area (Blocks and Districts)	Number of Respondents Below 18 years	18-45 years	Above 45years	Total
1.	Paramakudi	2	58	15	75
2.	Kamuthi	0	54	21	75
	Ramnathapuram	2	112	36	150
3.	Vasudevanallur	3	66	6	75
4.	Keelapavoor	1	60	14	75
	Tirunelveli Kattabomman	4	126	20	150
	Total Respondents	6	238	56	300
	Percentage	2.0	79.33	18.67	100

Source: Computed from primary data.

2. Sex

The sexwise classification of the sample respondents are presented in Table 4. It is clear from the table that of the 300 total sample respondents, 285 respondents (95 percent) are women and the study covered only 15 men respondents (5 percent). The study assumed that the women in India are comparatively more responsible in child bearing and rearing and the fertility rate in a family. Based on the assumption, the study covered a majority of women respondents through purposive random sampling method.

TABLE: 4
Sexwise classification of Sample Respondents

Sl. No.	Block and study Area - Districts	Male	Female	Total
1.	Paramakudi	3	72	75
2.	Kamuthi	1	74	75
	Ramnathapuram	4	146	150
3.	Vasudevanallur	5	70	75
4.	Keelapavoor	6	69	75
	Tirunelveli Kattabomman	11	139	150
	Total Respondents	15	285	300
	Percentage	5	95	100

Source: Computed from primary data.

3. Community

The community and religion of the PLC learners are the factors influencing the development of population education. The community and religion wise distribution of the sample respondents are exhibited in Table 4.

The table 5 showed that the majority of the respondents are Hindus (84 Percent) and a meagre percentage belong to Christians (16 percent). The sample respondents covered (the 40.66 percent) 122 scheduled caste (32.67 percent) 98 Most Backward, (25 percent) 75 Backward and (1.67 percent) 5 forward community. The study revealed that there is a domination of scheduled caste and Hindus in the literacy campaign. This depressed class of respondents are suitable for the reliable and analytical findings in the KAP study.

TABLE 5

Community and Religion wise Break-up of sample Respondents

Sl. No.	Community and Religion	Ramnathapuram		Tirunelveli Kattabomman		Total	Percentage
		Paramakudi	Kamuthi	Vasudevanallur	Keelapavoor		
1.	Hindu	59	68	68	57	252	84
2.	Christian	16	7	7	18	48	16
		75	75	75	75	300	100
3.	Forward	3	0	0	2	5	1.67
4.	Backward	9	19	23	24	75	25.00
5.	Most Backward	35	18	15	30	98	32.67
6.	Scheduled Caste	28	38	37	19	122	40.66
	Total	75	75	75	75	300	100.00

Source: Computed from Primary data.

4. Occupation:

Table 6 gives the occupational distribution of sample learners. Of the 300 sample respondents, 165 respondents (55 percent) had done the non-agricultural work and the 97 respondents (32.33 percent) were involved in the agricultural activities are handloom, Bricks, and Charcoal in Ramnathapuram district and Beedi works in Tirunelveli Kattabomman district. The women respondents are mainly involved in these non-agricultural activities.

TABLE 6

Occupationwise Distribution of the sample respondents

Sl. No.	Blocks and District	Cultivation	Agricultural labour	Non-Agricultural labour	others	Total
1.	Paramakudi	12	17	41	5	75
2.	Kamuthi	6	19	43	7	75
	Ramnathapuram	18	36	84	12	150
3.	Vasudevanallur	21	6	29	19	75
4.	Keelapavoor	5	11	52	7	75
	Tirunelveli Kattabomman	26	17	81	26	150
	Total	44	53	165	38	300
	Percentage	14.67	17.67	55.0	12.66	100

Source: Computed from primary data.

5. Annual Income

According to the Planning Commission, poverty line is described as the family having the average annual income of Rs.6400 or below the level. The study revealed that of the total sample respondents, 162 respondents (54.0 percent) are living below the poverty line and the average annual income of the respondents are Rs.7503. Their results are given in Table 7.

TABLE-7

Average Annual Income of the Sample Respondents

Sl. Blocks and Districts	Number of families having income		Average Annual Income (Rs.)
	Below Rs.6400	Above Rs.6400	
1. Paramakudi	32	43	7623
2. Kamuthi	48	27	8137
Ramnathapuram	80	70	7880
3. Vasudevanallur	39	36	7235
4. Keelapavoor	43	32	7017
Tirunelveli Kattabomman	82	68	7126
Total	162	138	7503
Percentage	54	46	

Source : Computed from primary data.

6. Type of Family and Housing Conditions:

The success of the population education project depends on the type of family and housing conditions of the beneficiaries. The sample Post Literacy Learner's type of family and housing conditions are exhibited in Table 4.6. It is clear from the table that majority of the sample learners (92.67 percent) are followed the nuclear family type and 66.33 percent of the respondents are having the own house. The electrified houses are 137 (45.67 percent) and 129 sample respondents (43 percent) are living in their huts.

TABLE 8:
Type of Family and Housing conditions of the sample respondents

Sl. No.	Districts	Type of Family Joint Nuclear	Housing Own-ed	Rented	Elec-trified	Not Electrified	huts	condition Kutched Pucca	
1.	Ramnathapuram	13	137	96	54	89	61	76	74
2.	Tirunelveli Kattabomman	9	141	103	47	48	102	53	97
	Total	22	278	199	101	137	163	129	171
	percentage	7.33	92.67	66.33	53.67	45.67	54.33	45	57

Source: computed from primary data.

The foregoing socio-economic profile of the respondents, i.e., mostly women, in high reproductive age group, belonging to the most backward and scheduled caste communities earning low income, large number of non-agricultural labourers, nuclear family system and non-electrified Kutcha house conditions, revealed the favourable conditions for the implementation of population education message through the literacy campaigns in the study district. It is seen that the study covered the appropriate sample learners in two district of Tamil Nadu.

B. The Knowledge and the Attitudes of the Respondents:

Under Post Literacy Campaign, Population education messages are spread to the learners through various reading materials and discussions in the centres. The knowledge about the population education is one of the important factor which helps the learners to take right type of decisions. The population issues like Age of marriage, Family Planning methods, Spacing of children, supplementary diets and Medical check-up during pregnancy, Women education, Girls's marriage and abortion are considered under this present study. The knowledge and attitude of the level of respondents on the above said population issues are presented in Table. 9 and 10.

1. Age of Marriage

Earlier marriage are common in India. Raising the minimum age of marriage is inherently desirable to improve the social climate in India, quite apart from its beneficent effects on population growth. The minimum age at marriage for girls, fixed at 14 by the Child Marriage Restraint Act of 1929, was raised to 15 in 1957 as part of the revision of the Hindu code involving a revision of the Hindu personal law. Consumation of marriage at an early age adversely affects health, especially of the girl. With this consideration, the Indian law has provided a minimum legal age for marriage of boys (24 years) and girls (21 years) before which a marriage is considered to be illegal.

TABLE-9

Knowledge of Respondents about some Population Issues

Sl. No.	Population Issues	Agreed/ correct Response Frequency	Disagreed/ Incorrect Response Frequency	Total Respo-nse Frequency	No Idea/ No Response
1.	Minimum Legal age of Boys and Girls	121 (40.33)	32 (10.67)	153 (51)	147 (49)
2.	Problems of Girls' Early Marriage	90 (30)	61 (20.330	151 (50.33)	149 (49.7)
3.	Family planning improve the quality of life	106 (35.33)	48 (16)	154 (51.33)	146 (48.67)
4.	Small Family leads to happy life	140 (46.67)	97 (32.33)	237 (79)	63 (21)
5.	Over population leads to scarcity of facilities	180 (60)	46 (15.33)	226 (75.33)	74 (24.67)
6.	Medical checkup of pregnant Mothers	105 (35)	161 (53.67)	266 (88.67)	34 (11.33)
7.	Supplementary diet during pregnancy	97 (32.33)	116 (38.67)	213 (71)	87 (29)
8.	Closely spaced child birth spoil the health of the Mothers	85 (28.33)	39 (13)	124 (41.33)	176 (58.67)
9.	More food to male child to grow	120 (40)	38 (12.67)	158 (52.67)	142 (47.33)
10.	Literacy is necessary for women to improve their status	151 (50.33)	58 (19.33)	209 (69.67)	91 (30.33)
11.	Married women getting an abortion to prevent an unwanted child	102 (34)	116 (38.67)	218 (72.67)	82 (27.33)

Source : Computed from primary data.
Note : Figures within Parenthesis denotes percentages.

TABLE-10

Knowledge of Respondents about population issues in two study districts

Sl. No.	Population Issues	Agreed/Correct Responses Frequency		Disagreed/ Incorrect Response Frequency		Total Respon-ses freque-ncy	No Responses	No idea	
		RD	TK	RD	TK	RD	TK	RD	TK
1.	Minimum Legal Age of Boys and Girls	52	69	14	18	66	87	84	63
2.	Problems of Girls Early Marriage	32	58	33	28	65	86	85	64
3.	Family Planning improve the quality of life	53	53	19	29	72	82	78	68
4.	Small Family Leads to a happy life	61	79	60	37	121	116	29	34
5.	Over population leads to scarcity of facilities	83	97	23	23	106	120	44	30
6.	Medical check-up of Pregnant Mother	50	55	83	78	133	133	17	17
7.	Supplementary Diet during Pregnancy	51	46	56	60	107	106	43	44
8.	Closely spaced child birth spoil the health of the Mother	39	46	21	18	60	64	90	86
9.	More food for Male child to Grow	52	68	19	19	71	87	79	63
10.	Literacy is necessary for women to improve their status	68	83	41	27	109	110	51	40
11.	Married women getting an abortion to prevent the unwanted child	59	43	52	74	111	117	39	43

Source : Computed from primary data

RD : Ramnathapuram District

TK : Tirunelveli Kattabomman District.

It is clear from the Table 9 that 40.33 percent of the respondents had correct knowledge of minimum legal age of marriage of girls (21 years) and boys (24 years). The rest of 10.67 percent learners gave the incorrect responses about minimum legal age. The 30 percent of the respondents (90) are aware of the problems of Girls' marriage at younger age and 61 respondents (20.33 percent) are not clear about the problems. Nearly 49 percent of the respondents in the study districts did not give any response (no idea) about this age of marriage issue. This result shows that only 51 percent of the post literacy learners in the Ramnathapuram and Tirunelveli Kattabomman districts are aware about the age of marriage and the problems.

2. Girls' Early Marriage:

The study analysed the respondent's knowledge about the effects of early marriage on girls. The findings of the study showed (Table 11) that the 151 respondents (50.33 percent) are aware of one or the other ill effects of early marriage of girls. The average number of responses of a respondent is 2.22. The responses are higher (29.85 percent) for the problem of early marriage leads to the birth of unhealthy children and 21.79 percent responses for the more chance of death of either mother or child at the time of delivery. It is inferred that nearly fifty percent of the PLC learner do not know the ill effects of the girls early marriage, this will lead to the population problem in the study districts.

The knowledge and opinion or the suggestions for improving the marriage age of girls were also gathered in the present study. The study revealed that of the 300 sample PLC learners, 161 learners (53.67 percent) did not make any suggestions and they were not aware about improving the marriage age of the girls. The rest of 139 respondents (46.33 percent) suggested the measures which formed the 273 frequency responses. It is inferred that providing education and employment opportunities for girls would definitely improve the marriage age of girls in the study districts. These facts are presented in Table 12.

TABLE-11

Knowledge of the Respondents on the Problems of Girls early Marriage

Sl. No.	Problems of Early Marriage	Frequency of Responses			Percentage
		Ramnad	T.K.	Total	
1.	Lead to birth of unhealthy children	44	56	100	29.85
2.	chances are more for the death of either Mother or child at the time of delivery	39	34	73	21.79
3.	Girl is not mature to take care of the family	20	29	55	26.42
4.	Early Marriage leads to more children	28	33	61	18.21
5.	Girl is deprived of education	13	19	32	9.55
6.	Any other	6	8	14	4.18
	Total	156	179	335	100
	Number of Respondents aware of the problems	65	86	151	50.33
	Average Number of responses	2.4	2.08	2.22	

Source: Computed from primary data.

TABLE-12

Knowledge/opinion of the Respondents to improve Marriage Age of girls

Sl. No.	Measures/Suggestions	Frequency of Responses			Percentage
		Ram-nad	T.K.	Total	
1.	Providing Education Facilities for girls nearby	49	53	102	37.36
2.	Providing Employment Opportunities for girls	63	54	117	42.86
3.	Improving Economic Status of the family	19	21	40	14.65
4.	Any other	8	6	14	5.13
	Total	139	134	273	100
5.	Don't know (Number of respondents)	87	74	161	53.67

Source: Computed from primary data.

3. Use of Family Planning:

In order to find out the knowledge level of the sample learners about the use and the need of family planning, three statements were given during the interview period. They are (a) Family Planning imporves the quality of life, (b) Small Family leads to happy life; and (c) Over population leads to scarcity of facilities. The acceptance or non-acceptance of these statements are gathered. The study found that 35.33 percent (106) and 46.67 percent (140) of the respondents had agreed the concepts viz., Family planning improves the quality of life and small family leads to happy life respectively. The 60 percent (180) of respondents are aware of the effect of over population on the scarcity of facilities. The 15.33 percent supported the over- population issues in the study districts. It is concluded that majority of the respondents acquired knowledge about the use and need of family planning. This level of knowledge will induce the PLC learners to adopt the various family planning measures.

4. Knowledge About Family Planning Methods:

According to National Family Health Survey 1992-93, in India, 96 percent of currently married women know about at least one contraceptive method, and 89 percent know where they go to obtain a modern method. Knowledge of family planning is nearly universal in Tamily Nadu. Currently married women are most familiar with female sterilization (99 percent), followed by male sterlization (86 percent), the IUD (78 percent), the pill (75 percent) and the condom (61 percent). Injection is the least heard-of method (13 percent). Traditional methods of contraception are known to 46 percent of women, with periodic abstinence and withdrawal known to 39 and 24 percent respectively.

The family planning methods such as Tubectomy, laprascope, coper 'T', oral pills, and condom are popularised through the doctors, health visitors, primary Health centres, Arivoli Iyyakkam, Television and Radio etc. The source of knowledge of the respondents about the family planning methods are also tested in this study. The findings are given in Table 13.

TABLE: 13

Awareness and source of awareness of Respondents on the Family Planning Methods:

Sl. No.	Source	Number of Respondents knowing Family planning							Percentage
		Ramnad one method	More than one methord	T.K one method	More than one methord	Total one method	More than one methord	Total Respo-ndents	
1.	Doctor	2	1	7	5	9	6	15	8.48
2.	Health Visitor	32	12	29	11	61	23	84	47.46
3.	Primary Health Centre	5	3	4	2	9	5	14	7.91
4.	Friends	6	5	8	5	14	10	24	13.56
5.	Relatives	3	0	3	2	6	2	8	4.52
6.	Spouse	3	4	5	2	8	6	14	7.91
7.	Arivoli Iyyakkam	0	2	0	4	0	6	6	3.39
8.	Television/Radio	1	2	1	3	2	5	7	3.95
9.	Others	1	0	2	2	3	2	5	2.82
	Total	53	29	59	36	112	65	177	100

Source: Computed from primary data.

It is clear from the table 13 that of the total sample respondents, 177 (59 percent) respondents are knowing about the family planning methods in the study districts. The 112 respondents (37.33 percent) are knowing any one method and 65 respondents (21.67 percent) are aware of the one more methods. The church fathers advised the christians to have only two children in a family in Ramnathapuram district. In most of the villages Grama Sevak (Thalaiyari) create the awareness about the family planning methods. Regarding the source of awareness about the family planning methods, Health visitor had played an important role in the two study districts. It is inferred that 41 percent of the PLC learners did not know about the family planning methods. The literacy campaign had failed to create the awareness about these methods and the health visitors took the necessary steps to spread the population education message to the respondents in the study districts.

5. Maternal and child care:

Maternal care is a term used to refer the care of the pregnant women, care at delivery and care during the immediate period after the delivery of the child. Such care is of course a vital issue as a large part of infant mortality and a considerable part of infant mortality is related to the quality of such services available. The study attempts to find out the knowledge and attitude of the PLC learners in the study districts on the basis of the six important issues relating to the maternal and child care. They are: a) Medical check up of Pregnant Mother, b) Supplementary diet during Pregnancy, c) closely spaced child birth and mother health; d) More food for male child; e) Literacy for women to improve their status and f) Abortion to prevent the unwanted child.

The crises of child birth can be drastically reduced by going to the nearest health worker for regular check ups during pregnancy. Tables 9 and 10 showed that 35 percent (105) of the responses are in favour for undertaking the medical check up and 53.67 percent (161) did not agree the medical check up during the pregnancy. It is clear that a large number of pregnant mother did not want to take medical check up in the study districts due to many reasons such as lack of awareness, lack of facilities, money and time constraints etc. Their attitude towards the medical check up was also very poor in this study districts.

All women need more food during pregnancy. All pregnant women need more rest. The study found that (Table 9) only 32.33 percent of the respondents are known about the need for the supplementary diets during pregnancy. The 39.67 percent sample learners disagreed the issue of supplementary diets and 29 percent (87) had no idea about this supplementary diet. It is clear that in the study districts, the one third of the PLC learners got the positive knowledge and the attitude towards the supplementary diets to the mothers for the maternal and child care during the pregnancy.

Spacing pregnancies at least two years above, and avoiding pregnancies below the age of 18 or above the age of 35, drastically reduces the dangers of child bearing. Proper spacing of children has a direct link with health of the mother. In closer births, the parents and especially the mother, is unable to give the desired care and attention to her children. Also, the proper spacing of children reduces the possibilities of total births in the reproductive life span. The knowledge of respondents about spacing of their child birth was measured in this study.

The results showed (Table 9) that only 28.33 percent (85) of the respondent agreed that the closely spaced child birth spoil the health of the mother and 13 percent (39) disagreed the issue. A large number of (176) respondents did not give any responses (no idea) about this issue. It is found that the majority of the PLC learners in the study districts did not have the knowledge about the spacing of child birth population issue and the relation to the natural case. This level of knowledge do not help the respondents to improve the family planning practices for spacing the child birth.

The 40 percent of the respondents reported that more food is needed to grow the male child and 12.67 percent provided the incorrect responses on this issue. The 47.33 percent (142) respondents do not aware about the issue of more food for male child. It is found that 60 percent of the PLC learners did not know issue of more food for male child to grow and this will affect the growth of the children in the study area.

Maternal care must be seen as part of addressing the entire issues of women's health concerns. Women's health itself is only a specific dimension of the larger issue of gender equity. The entire approach to health education for women including maternal care and family planning must be addressed as a process of empowering women with knowledge and skills so that she can make the right choices.

Based on this consideration, the knowledge of the respondents on the issue that 'Literacy is necessary for women to improve their status' was measured. The result showed that the correct and incorrect responses about this issue was 50.33 percent (151) and 19.33 percent (58) respectively. The 50 percent of the PLC learners in the study districts understand and agreed importance of education for women for their development of socio and economic status.

Abortion was made a crime for which the mother as well as the abortionist could be punished in all cases except where it had to be induced in order to save the mother's life. But, unfortunately, usually neither the average doctor nor the mother is aware of the law that permits threapentic abrotion with the result that very few abortions have been carried out in Government or private hospital. On the other hard, abortion could be possible only, with the acceptance of the pregnant mothers. The knowledge of the respondents on the issue that the married women getting an abortion to prevent an unwanted child, was measured in the study area.

The study found that (Table 9) the agreed, disagreed and no responses of the respondents are 34 percent (102), 38.67 percent (116) and 27.33 percent (82) respectively. It is undeniable fact that one third of the PLC learners (Indian Mothers) are prepared to risk their lives in an illegal abortion rather than carry that particular child, i.e., unwanted child to term.

6. Attitude towards sex preference:

The findings of the National Family Health survey, 1992-93 revealed that preference for sons is not very strong in Tamil Nadu. To the extent that it exists, it is stronger in rural areas than in urban areas. Among women who do not have any children, 15 percent want a son, 6 percent want a daughter, 65 percent say it does not matter, and 15 percent say it is upto God for their first child. The present study attempts to findout the sex preference of the PLC learners in the Ramnathapuram and Tirunelveli Kattabomman districts. The sex preference of the respondents are exhibited in Table 14.

TABLE-14

Sex preference of the sample respondents:

Sl. No.	preference particulars	Number of Respondents Prefered			Percen-tage
		Ramnad	T.K.	Total	
1.	To have first child male	51	56	107	35.67
2.	To have first child female	13	17	30	10.0
3.	No preference	86	77	163	54.33
4.	Importance atleast to have one son				
	a) Very Important	93	106	199	66.33
	b) Some what Impoȝtant	28	34	62	20.67
	c) Unimportant	29	10	39	13.0
5.	Importance atleast to have one daughter				
	a) Very Important	16	21	37	12.33
	b) Some what Important	17	13	30	10.0
	c) Unimportant	117	116	233	77.67
6.	Prefer to equal division of property	20	28	48	16.0

Source: Computed for primary data.

The study found that 54.33 percent of the sample respondents did not have the preferences in sex in the study districts. The 35.67 percent (107 respondents) preferred to have the first child male and 66.33 percent respondents gave importance atleast to have one son in a family. The majority of the respondents (77.67 percent) gave the unimportance at least to have one daughter. Most of the parents expected that male children would be helpful to the parent's occupation in the study areas. It is inferred that the PLC learners in study districts gave more preference to male sex than the female sex among their children. But only 16 percent of the respondents (48) prefer to equal division of their properties. They also emphasised that after completing the marriage expenses for girls, the property are to be distributed to the male children.

C. Family Welfare and Health practices:

The knowledge related to the population issues like marriage age, ill effects of early marriage, family planning methods, maternal and child care, abortion of unwanted child, would help the sample respondents to rationalise the thinking favorable for population control measures. The attitude of the PLC learners towards the preference of number of children and a spefic sex and other health care methods would also be determined by the level of knowledge.

Under this KAP study, the success of the population education activities depend mainly on the practice of the sample respondents on the family welfare and health in the study districts of Tamil Nadu. This section attempts to analyse the family welfare and health practices of the PLC learners in Ramnathapuram and Tirunelveli Kattabomman districts.

1. Age of Marriage:

In a country like India, where early marriage is preferred, this factor assumes more significance for demographers and population planners. Bearing of children immediately after marriage is also preferred and encourage in most of the Indian families. This preference added to early marriage, poses severe threat to the mother as well as child. At the time of National Family Health Survey in India (1992-93). 39 percent of women (age 15-19) were married and 95 percent of women (age 25-29) were married. Marriages at very young ages have been declining drastically overtime. Although marriage is relatively late, it is nearly universal in Tamil Nadu. The singulate mean age at marriage is 26.4 years for males and 20.5 years for female. The medium age first marriage for women age 20-49 is 18.3 years. Among women age 30-34, only 3 percent have never married.

The age at marriage of the sample respondents of the study are exhibited in Table 15. From the table, it is clear that the 54.67 percent of the respondents got married between the age of 18 years and 25 years and the 36.33 percent got the early marriage at the age of below 18 years. The early marriage was higher in the Ramnathapuram district (63) than the Tirunelveli Kattabomman district (46). Only 27 respondents (9 percent) got the marriage above the 25 years and the same marriage age group was comparatively higher in the Tirunelveli Kattabomman district than the Ramanathapuram district.

TABLE 15
Age at marriage of the respondents in the studyDistricts

Sl. No.	Blocks and Districts	Number of Respondents Age at Marriage			
		Below 18 years	18 to 25 years	Above 25 years	Total
1.	Paramakudi	31	40	4	75
2.	Kamuthi	32	40	3	75
	Ramnathapuram	63	80	7	150
3.	Vasudevanallur	20	46	9	75
4.	Keelapavoor	26	38	11	75
	Nellai Kattabomman	46	84	20	150
	Total	109	164	27	300
	Percentage	36.33	54.67	9.0	100

Source: Computed from primary data.

It is inferred that the practice of early marriage was prevailing more in Ramnathapuram districts due to many factors. The reasons for early marriage of their daughters are given in Table 16.

The table 16 revealed that majority of the parents did the marriage for their daughters at an early age due to the main reasons such as availability of relative groom, getting married in their working place, not obliging the parent's control and fulfilling the social responsibility by agents. These reasons secured the first three ranks in the study districts.

TABLE-16
Reason for practicing Early Marriage of Girls:

Sl.	Reasons	Response Ramnad	Frequency T.K	Total	Percentage	Rank
1.	Non-Availability of higher education facilities nearby	29	16	45	4.99	9
2.	Fear of Pre-Marital sex	38	44	82	9.10	4
3.	Difficulty in getting a suitable groom	26	20	46	5.11	8
4.	Problem of more dowry with increased age	37	41	78	8.66	5
5.	Fulfilling social responsibility by parents	46	56	102	11.32	3
6.	Girls were not good at studies	17	9	26	2.89	11
7.	Availability of relative groom	88	91	179	19.87	1
8.	Due to poor economic status	33	26	59	6.55	7
9.	Due to high economic status	15	11	26	2.88	12
10.	More than one matured girl at home	48	27	75	8.32	6
11.	Any other - occupational situation and parent's uncontrol	76	63	139	15.43	2
12.	Do not know the reason	19	25	44	4.88	10
	Total frequency	472	429	901	100	

Source : Computed from primary data.

2. Practice of Family planning:

As per the National Family and Health Survey 1992-93, forty one percent of commonly married women age 15-19 in India, practicing family planning 37 percent use a modern contraceptive method, 4 percent use a traditional method. Only 41 percent of married women commonly use family planning. Female sterlization is the most commonly used method of family planning. In Tamil Nadu, 50 percent of married women age 15-49 years are commonly using a contraceptive method, with 45 percent using a modern method and 5 percent using traditional method. Female sterlization is the most popular method (38 percent) followed by the IUD (4 percent), Male sterlization (2 percent), the condom (2 percent) and the pill (less than

1 percent) are much less popular. Overall, the use of spacing methods is very low.

The findings of the study in Ramnathapuram and Tirunelveli Kattabomman Districts relating to the practice of Family Planning methods, decision making in adopting the methods and the reasons for non-adopting the methods are presented in Tables 17, 18. 19, 20 and 21 respectively.

It is clear from the Table 17 that of the 300 sample respondents, 101 respondents (33.67 percent) were adopting the family planning methods. Tubectomy (22.77 percent), Laprascope (27.72 percent) and Coper 'T' (29.71 percent), are the popular methods among the PLC learners. A meagre percentage of respondents are using the oral pills (4.95 percent) condom (8.91 percent) and other (5.94 percent) in the study districts.

TABLE 17

Practice of Family Planning Methods by the sample Respondents

Sl. No.	Practised Methods	Number of Respondents			Percentage
		Ramnad	N.K.	Total	
1.	Vasectomy	-	-	-	-
2.	Tubectomy	13	10	23	22.77
3.	Laprascope	12	16	28	27.72
4.	Coper 'T'	11	19	30	29.71
5.	Oral Pills	1	4	5	4.95
6.	Condom	3	6	9	8.91
7.	Others	4	2	6	5.94
	Total	44	57	101	100

Source: computed from primary data.

The study found that of the total family planning adopters, 33.66 percent respondents adopted the methods after getting two to three childrens. The adopters having 3 to 4 children are 30.69 percent of the respondents. Only 9.9 percent respondents adopted the family planning methods after getting the one children. This type of practice commonly used for spacing of the child birth in the study districts.

TABLE-18

Practice of Family Planning Methods by the respondents.

Sl. No.	Blocks and Districts	Number of Respondents Practiced Family Planning during					
		At present	First-2 child	2to 3 child	3-4 child	4& above	Total
1.	Paramakudi	2	1	6	7	4	20
2.	Kamuthi	1	2	7	9	5	14
	Ramnathapuram	3	1	6	7	4	20
3.	Vasudevanallur	2	2	11	8	3	26
4.	Keelapavoor	4	5	0	7	5	31
	Nellai Kattabomman	6	7	21	15	8	57
	Total	9	10	34	31	17	101
	Percentage	8.91	9.9	33.66	30.69	16.83	33.67

Source: Computed from Primary data.

It is inferred that the use of contraception is highest among women with two or three children. The 19 adopters (18.81 percent) in the study districts are suffering from some problems after adopting the family planning methods. The study revealed that 71.29 percent (72) adopters received the contraceptives from the public sector at free of cost and the rest of 28.71 percent (29) adopters from the private sector nurshing homes and private doctors. These figures are given in Table 19.

TABLE 19:

Source of Practice of Family Planning and Post adoption problems of the Respondents.

Sl.	Particulars/Source	Number of Family Palnning adopters			Percentage
		Ramnad	T.K	Total	
1.	Practice of Family Planning through public sector at free cost	29	43	72	71.29
2.	Practice of Family Planning through Private Sector	18	11	29	28.71
3.	Problems after Practising family planning	13	6	19	18.81

Source: Computed from primary data.

Role of women in decision making regarding adoption of family planning methods is very important. Because, it is the woman who has to bear the maximum burden of bearing and rearing of children. The study found that in the study districts, 37.62 percent of the family planning adopter's spouse had taken decision on the practice of the methods. The 28.71 percent of adopters took their own decision and the 24 (23.76 percent) elders of the adopters took the decision. It is inferred that spouse (husband) dominated in taking the decision of family planning practice among the PLC learners in the study districts.

TABLE-20

Decision making person in practicing Family planning methods

Sl. No.	Decision Making Persons	No.of Respondents Ramnad	T.K	Total	Percentage
1.	Respondent	9	20	29	28.71
2.	Spouse	21	17	38	37.62
3.	Elders	8	16	24	23.76
4.	Others	6	4	10	9.91
	Total	44	57	101	100

Source: computed from primary data.

The study observed that of the total 300 sample respondents, 177 (59 percent) are aware about the family planning methods (Table 4.11), but only 101 (33.67 percent) respondents were practised the methods. The rest of 199 (66.33 percent) respondents do not adopt the family planning methods in the study area. The reasons for non-practising the methods are discussed in Table 21.

It is seen from the table 21 that fear of side effects of contraceptives (24.12 percent) want of specific sex children and additional children (52.76 percent) are the main reasons for not practicing the family planning methods in the study districts. Only 9.55 percent of the respondents revealed the reasons as that the elders/husband/family members are against the family planning methods. The cost of contraceptives also affect the 10.55 percent of the respondents.

TABLE-21

Reasons for not practising the Family planning methods in the study Area

Sl. No.	Decision Making Persons	No.of Respondents Ramnad	T.K	Total	Percen tage
1.	Lack of knowledge	2	4	6	3.02
2.	For want of additional children	13	16	29	14.57
3.	Elders/Husband/Family Members are against it	14	5	19	9.55
4.	Against the religion	-	-	-	-
5.	Fear of side effects	27	21	48	24.12
6.	Cost of contraceptives	9	12	21	10.55
7.	Other reasons-newly married, want of child of specific sex	41	35	76	38.19
	Total	106	93	199	100

Source: Computed from Primary data.

From the field survey, the study found out some other reasons for not adopting the family planning methods in the study areas are: (i) The nature of hard work in the agricultural fields created some problems after adopting the sterilization; (ii) Illhealth like Tuberculosis etc. restrict the adoption of methods; (iii) Not necessary of adopting the contraceptives due to the stop of bleeding at the early reproductive age; and (iv) Some women wants to adopt sterlization at the time of delivery and not good health at the time of delivery.

3.Family Size

The size of the family was surveyed in the two study districts. The results are exhibited in Table 22. The table revealed that the total number of male, female and children in 300 respondent's family in two districts are 454, 445, and 330 respectively. The average number of persons in a family is 1.51 male, 1.48 female and 5.92 children.

TABLE-22
Size of the Family of the Respondents:

Sl. No.	Blocks and Districts	Total Number of persons Male	Female	Children
1.	Paramakudi	136	89	124
2.	Kamuthi	113	162	101
	Ramnathapuram	249	251	225
3.	Vasudevanallur	90	99	148
4.	Keelapavoor	115	95	119
	Tirunelveli Kattabomman	205	194	267
	Total	454	445	492
	Average Number of persons in a family	1.51	1.48	5.92

Source: Computed from Primary data.

The study found that 57 percent of the respondents in the study districts are having 2 and below children in a family and only 26 percent are having more than 2 chidren in a family. The 17 percent of the sample learners do not have any children at present. It is inferred that the small family norms are practised by the large number of PLC learners in these districts.

4. Infant and child mortality:

According to the National Family and Health Survey 1992-93, infant and child mortality have declined substantially in the last 15 year. Between age 1 and 5 years, females experiences 43 percent higher mortality risks than males. In Tamil nadu, the infant morality rate for the five year (1987-91) period immediately preceding the survey is estimated to be 68 per 1000 live births, child mortality (age 1-4) is 20 per 1000, and under five mortality is 87 per 1000. Infant and child mortality declined steadily during the last 15 years, but 12 children still dies before reaching the fifth birthday.

Table-23

Rate of children in a respondent's family:

Sl. No.	Blocks and Districts	Family without children	Family Below 2	Having Above 2	children Total
1.	Paramakudi	16	43	16	59
2.	Kamuthi	15	44	16	60
	Ramnathapuram	31	67	32	119
3.	Vasudevanallur	13	35	27	62
4.	Keelapavoor	7	49	19	68
	Tirunelveli Kattabomman	20	84	46	130
	Total	51	171	78	249
	Percentage	17	57	26	83

Source : Computed from primary data.

The infant (0 to 1 years) and child (1 to 12 years) mortality rate under the present study are exhibited in Table 24 and Table 25.

TABLE-24

Infant and child Mortality in study districts:

Sl. No.	Details	Mortality in sample Respondent's family Ramnad	T.K.	Total
1.	Infant Mortality (0 to 1 years)	14	11	25
2.	Child Mortality (1 to 12 years)	12	19	31
	Total	26	30	56

Source: Computed from primary data.

Table 25 revealed that the infant and child mortality was 56 in the 300 respondent's family. The infant and child mortality rate is 102.19 in the study districts i.e., 102.19 deaths per 1000 born children in the respondent's family. The rate includes the infant (0-1 years) and child (1-12 years) mortality in two districts. The common causes of infant and childhood mortality in India are diarrohocal diseases, acute upper respiratory infections, viral exanthemata like measles, malaria and intestinal parasites as well as neonatal tetanus.

In the study areas, the infant Mortality was caused due to the death at the time of and after delivery, low birth weight, early delivery child (predisposition) and diarrhoea. The child mortality (1-11 years) was occurred due to diarrohoea, small pox, malaria and other fevers. It is inferred that the infant under 1 year of age, the death was account for 82 percent in the Ramnathpuram and Tirunelveli Kattaboman districts.

TABLE-25

Infant and Child Mortality Rate in the study districts.

Sl. No.	Blocks and Districts	No.of child ever born			No of child died			Number of child at present		
		M	F	Total	M	F	Total	M	F	Total
1.	Paramakudi	62	66	128	1	8	9	61	58	119
2.	Kamuthi	67	56	123	8	9	17	59	47	106
	Ramnathapuram	129	122	251	9	17	26	120	105	225
3.	Vasudevanallur	75	66	141	9	9	18	66	57	123
4.	Keelapavoor	74	82	156	8	4	12	66	78	144
	Tirunelveli	278	270	548	26	30	56	252	240	492

Source: Computed from primary data. M - Male; F- Female

5. Maternal care and Delivery:

The report of the National Family Health survey 1992-93 revealed that in India, 49.1 percent of births whose mothers received antenatal care from a doctor or other health professional and 53.8 percent received 2 or more tetanus taxoid injections. The 74 percent of babies are delivered at home and only 34 percent of deliveries are assisted by a doctor or a nurse/midwife.

The survey report showed that coverage by antenatal care and delivery care services in Tamil Nadu is among the best in the country. Mothers received antenatal care for 94 percent of their births during the four years preceding the survey. Mothers in rural areas are less likely than mothers in urban areas to visit a health institution or antenatal care. Ninty percent of mothers who gave birth during the last four years received two doses of tetanus taxoid vaccination during their pregnancy.

The present study analysed the maternal care relating to the supplement foods and Medical check up during last pregnancy and the details in the study districts. The findings of the maternal care are given in tables 26, 27, 28 and 29. From the table 26, it is clear that 97 (34.03 percent) women respondents were taking supplements foods and 105 respondents (36.84 percent) were undergone the medical check up during their last pregnancy. It is inferred that only one third women respondents had practised in the maternal care activities in the study districts.

TABLE-26

Supplement foods and Medical check up during the last preganancy

Sl. No.	Blocks and Districts	Number of women Respondents practising	
		Supplement Foods	Medical check up
1.	Paramakudi	13	21
2.	Kamuthi	38	29
	Ramnathapuram	51	50
3.	Vasudevanallur	29	27
4.	Keelapavoor	17	28
	Tirunelveli Kattabomman	46	55
	Total	97	105
	Percentage	34.03	36.84

Source : Computed from primary data.

The study revealed that (Table 27), 54 women respondents got the medical asistance from Government and other Public Hospitals during the last pregnancy and 39 respondents practised medical check up in the private hospitals. Most of the women respondents had used the public facilities for the maternal care activities in the study districts.

TABLE-27

Source of Medical check up during the last pregnancy

Sl. No.	Place of check up	Ramnatha-puram	Tirunel-veli Katta-bomman	Total	Percent-age
1.	Public Hospitals	25	29	54	51.43
2.	Private Hospitals	17	22	39	57.14
3.	Others	8	4	12	11.43

Source: Computed from primary data.

TABLE-28

Periods of Medical check-up of their last pregnancy in the study districts.

Sl. No.	Period and Times	Ramnad	T.K	Total	Percentage
	During the period				
1.	Between 1 to 3 months	17	23	40	38.10
2.	Between 4 to 6 months	12	17	29	27.62
3.	Between 5 to 9 months	21	15	36	34.28
4.	Check up one Time	27	18	45	42.86
5.	" Two times	19	25	44	41.90
6.	" More than 2 times	4	12	16	15.24

Source : Computed from primary data.

TABLE-29

Details of Delivery

Sl. No.	Place of delivery	Ramnad	T.K	Total	Percentage
1.	Public Hospital	22	9	41	27.70
2.	Private Hospital	11	18	29	19.59
3.	House	48	29	67	45.27
4.	Others	5	6	11	7.43
	Total	86	62	148	100.00

Source: Computed from primary data.

In the study report, 47.29 percent of births occured with public and private health facilities. The 45.27 percent were attended by traditional birth attendents or other persons. It is reported that in the study districts, nearly fifty percent of women respondents birth were assisted by a doctor or nurse/midwife.

V.SUMMARY AND CONCLUSIONS;

In order to analyse the Knowledge, Attitude and Practise of the Neo-Literates on the specific reference to population education messages in Ramanathapuram and Tirunelveli Kattabomman Districts of Tamil Nadu, the data were collected from the 300 sample married respondents in the age group of 15 to 45. The findings of the study are summarised below:

1. The study covered the 79.33 percent of the respondents in the age group of 18 to 45 years and it consists of 285 male respondents (95 percent) and 15 female respondents (5 percent).
2. The 84 percent of the respondent belong to the Hindu religion and the 73.33 percent of the learners belong to the depressed community i.e., Scheduled Caste and Most Backward Caste.
3. The sample respondents are 53 agricultur .l labourers (17.67 percent) and 165 non-agricultural labourers (55 percent) in the study districts.
4. The study revealed that 162 respondents (54 percent) are living below the poverty line and the average annual income of the respondents is Rs. 7503.

5. Majority of the respondents (92.67 percent) are living in a nuclear family type and in their own houses (66.33 percent). The electrified houses are 137 (45.67 percent) and 129 sample respondents are living in the huts.
6. The 40.33 percent of the respondents had the correct knowledge of minimum legal age of marriage of girls and boys and only 30 percent of the respondents are aware of the problems of girls early marriage.
7. The 161 sample learners did not provide any suggestion for improving the marriage age and the rest of the respondents suggested to provide the education and employment.
8. The 112 respondents (37.33 percent) are knowing the any one method of the popular contraceptives and 65 respondents (21.67 percent) are aware of the one more methods. The total of 177 sample respondents are known the family planning methods.
9. Health visitor in the villages had played an important role in creating the awareness about the family planing methods.
10. The greater frequency of Pregnant Mothers responses (195 responses did not favour to take the medical check-up due to many reasons and only 32.33 percent of the respondents agreed to take the supplement foods during the last pregnancy.
11. Majority of the PLC learners in the study district do not have the knowledge about the spacing of child birth population issue and the relation to the maternal care.
12. It is undeniable fact that one third of 13 the PLC learners are prepared to risk their lives in all illegal abortion rather than carry that unwanted child.
13. The 35.67 percent preferred to have the first child male and 66.33 percent gave importance atleast to have one son in a family.
14. The 54.67 percent of the respondents got marriage between the age of 18 years and 25 years and the 36.33 percent got the early marriage at the age of below 18 years due to the availability of relative groom, occupational favourism and uncontrol of parents.
15. The 101 respondents (33.67 percent) were practising the family planning methods such as Tubectomy (22.77 percent), Laprascope (27.72 percent) and coper 'T' (29.71 percent). Of the total family planning adopters 33.66 percent respondents adopted the methods after getting two to three children.
16. The spouse of the adopters (37.62 percent) and the respondents (28.71 percent) are decision makers in practising family planning.

17. The main reasons for not practising the method are the fear of side effect and for the want of specific sex children
18. There are 25 infant Mortality (0-1 years) and 31 child Mortality (1-12 years) families in the study districts. The infant and child Mortality rate is 102.19 deaths per 1000 born children in the study districts.
19. Only one third of the women respondents had practised the maternal care activities in the study districts.
20. The 47.29 percent of births are occurred with public or private health facilities in the hospitals.

From the above discussions and findings, we may conclude that the population education message to the neo-literates of the Post Literacy Campaign must be communicated in the alternative effective methods. Since 51 percent of PLC learners are having the knowledge on family planning methods, only 33.67 percent of respondents are practising the contraceptives. The materials relating to population education messages must be prepared to the level of literacy of the PLC learners and the fear of side effects of the contraceptives may be cleared through the mass media communications like television.

6

LITERACY CAMPAIGN AND EMPOWERMENT

INTRODUCTION

In India, with five year plan, there has been a growing realisation at policy level that rural poverty and unemployment can not be mitigated with wage employment programmes like National Rural Employment Programme (NREP), Rural Landless Employment Guarantee Programme (RLEGP) and Jawahar Rozgar Yojana (JRY) and the rural development programmes like Integrated Rural Development Programme (IRDP) alone.

Lack of adequate attention to small and rural industries has led to large scale migration of population from the rural to urban areas in search of jobs. Concentration of industries in cities has, in turn, led to congestion and other problems, including pollution.

The mounting problem of employment has brought into focus the importance of small scale, agro and rural industries as well as development of entrepreneurship in the related fields.

Preliminary studies of the Planning Commission have emphasised that the potentials of this sector should be adequately tapped. Investment per job in this sector would be very low compared to the organised sector. Further, development of this sector would help dispersal of industrial activity reducing inequality and poverty. Development of this sector normally involves acceleration of entrepreneurship movement.

As far as the entrepreneurship development is concerned it may be mentioned that there is no shortage of inherent entrepreneurial talent in the country. What is necessary is to draw out this inherent potential to make the latest talent patent and on galvanise the men, women and the youth to work towards a harmonious blend of personal, corporate and national objective.

Compared to Government Organisation like District Industries Centre (DIC) and District Rural Development Agency (DRDA), the role of voluntary organisation in developing entrepreneurial skill is highly appreciable on account of numerous factors which associate with them. To cater to the needs of entrepreneurial development programme, a great amount of co-ordination among various agencies at work is all the more necessary and this alone can steer rural youth to success in their venture.

The learners of the literacy campaign in Madurai District formed a women organisation and named as "Arivoli Mahalir Iyyakkam" (AMI) for the development of entrepreneurial activities in rural areas. The present study attempts to evaluate the role of the organisation in the rural enterprise development in Madurai District of Tamil Nadu.

DESIGN OF THE STUDY

The specific objectives of the study are:

i. To study the growth and performance of Arivoli Mahalir Iyyakkam in Madurai District;
ii. To analyse the role of the Iyyakkam on the rural entrepreneurs development activities;
iii. To evaluate the successful implementation of DWCRA scheme on fair price shops, canteen, cooking powders and washing powders, rearing milch animals etc; and
iv. To suggest various concrete measures for the successful implementation of rural enterprise development in the district.

Based on the above objectives of the study, primary data as well as secondary data were collected in Madurai District. In order to find out the growth and performance of the "Arivoli Mahalir Iyyakkam" and achievements of the literacy campaign in the district, secondary data were collected from the "Madurai District Arivoli Iyyakkam" Office, Madurai and from the records of the Arivoli Mahalir Iyyakkam Office.

Primary data relating the rural enterprise development activities and impact of DWCRA assistance were collected by interview method. A total of 30 women groups were interviewed with pretested questionnaire. The major activities of the women group such as cooking powder preparation, washing products, fair price shops and canteen were given more importance in the survey period. The findings of the study are presented as the case study in Fair price shops, canteen, cooking powders, milk depots, and washing products.

RESULTS AND DISCUSSION

The findings of the study are presented in four sections. They are:-

1. Literacy campaign in Madurai District.
2. Growth and performance of Arivoli Mahalir Iyyakkam in Madurai District.
3. DWCRA Assistance for Arivoli Mahalir Iyyakkam, and
4. Case studies on Rural Enterprise development by Arivoli Mahalir Iyyakkam.

LITERACY CAMPAIGN IN MADURAI DISTRICT

The illiterates under the age group (15-35) in Tamil Nadu accounts for 5.87 millions. Total literacy campaign projects are covering over 7.45 million illiterates. This includes learners above 35 years also. The campaigns have been implemented in 21 districts. Of the 21 districts, post literacy campaign was completed in Kanyakumari, Kamarajar Pudukottai and Pasumpon Muthuramalingam District. Post Literacy Campaign is in the process of having implemented in 10 districts namely, Madurai, North Arcot, Ramanathapuram, Tirunelveli, Dindigul Anna and Coimbatore Districts.

The Achievement of Madurai District in the Total Literacy phase is 76.38 percent against the total ranges of 3.28 lakhs. Nearly 3.07 lakhs learners have been enrolled. Among them 2.50 lakhs learners have completed the level III. The target age group for the campaign is (15-35) as per the sanction by the Ministry.

In Madurai, Post Literacy Project was sanctioned in May 1993 to cover 1.80 lakhs Neo literates. As much as 1.35 lakh neo-literates are reportedly enrolled. About 1.08 lakh learners attended PLC as on May 1994. The approved cost for post literacy campaign is Rs.1.46 crores of which Rs.0.97 crores was sanctioned from National Literacy Mission and Rs.0.49 crores from the State Government.

The PLC in Madurai District was launched with the main intention of facilitating a continuous approach for after becoming literate, an adult generally becomes motivated to learn more things and shows more interest in reading different types of books and other published materials. He/She wants to use and develop his reading, writing skills. In general, he wants to learn more and continues the process of education. It was felt that if suitable learning opportunities are not provided the neo-literates may lapse back to illiteracy.

The major objective of the Post Literacy is to reinforce and consolidate the skills relating to literacy among the learners, and to equip the learners with better knowledge, perception, skills, attitude, understanding, awareness, functionality etc., of the surrounding society and the nation at large. So, they are equipped to remove the impediments coming in the way of leading a better, happier and more meaningful life that they become active members of the community and participate in the process of social reconstruction and national development.

In Madurai District, each Panchayat Union has one Block Project Co-ordinator (BPC), 2 Assistant Project Co-ordinators (APC) and one office assistant for the implementation of PLC at block level. There is a library in each panchayat maintained by the Panchayat Co-ordinator. The Panchayat Co-ordinator also co-orodinates and supervises the Centres (vattam) in the panchayat area. Generally each panchayat covers three to four centres which is guided by the Vatta Vazhikatti (Circle Guide). Based on these administrative and organisational background, the Vattam functions twice a week. The reading materials are supplied and circulated among Neo-literates among the Vattams. Many self help groups have been formulated in every Vattam of PLC in Madurai District.

ARIVOLI MAHALIR IYYAKKAM IN MADURAI DISTRICT

Arivoli Mahalir Iyyakkam-Tamil Name for the organisation of the women learners literacy campaign was formed on 8.3.1995 by the Neo-literates of Post Literacy campaign in Madurai District. The office address of the organisation is 16, Old Ramanathapuram District Collector's Office, Madurai - 625 020.

The Arivoli Mahalir Iyyakkam (AMI) was Officially registered under the Societies Registration Act of 1860 (TN Act 27 of 1975) at Madurai on 15.5.95. The Office bearers at the time of registration are as follows:

1. V.V.G Ganeswari - President, Mellur.
2. N. Vijayalakshmi - Vice President, Ellis Nagar.
3. S. Navanitham - Secretary, E. Kottaipatti.
4. S. Vijayalakshmi - Assistant Secretary, Kallikudi.
5. T. Thavamani Devi - Treasurer, Mellakkal.
6. G.Mallika - Executive Member, Allinagaram.
7. A. Puspham - Executive Member, Achampattu.

The Neo- literates of the Post-Literacy campaign are enrolled as members of the Organisation. The above 18 years girls are eligible to become the member of the society and they have to pay Rs. 2 as annual subscription. The specific aims of the Society are:-

i. To organise various groups in all villages of the Madurai District in order to implement various women development programmes;
ii. To help the members in maintaining the libraries, developing small savings, insurance and Government assistance for the women groups in Madurai District;
iii. To implement the various schemes like Educational For All, Health For all, Mother and child care, Women Development, Waste Land Development, Water Resource Management, Environmental Protection etc.;
iv. To provide training and assistance to develop the entrepreneurial skills of the women groups in villages to start the small scale industries;
v. To identify the marking potentialities for the women entrepreneurs;
vi. To generate employment opportunities for the members with non-Profit enterprises; and

vii. To develop the agro-based industries and to popularise the agricultural development schemes in the rural areas.

Under this AMI, at the initial stage, one women team was formed in each Panchayat. During the period of eight months (May 1995 to December 1995), nearly 240 women teams were organised in Madurai District. The 'Self-help' groups, at the beginning, start to save their excess income by opening an account in the near by bank (Joint A/C of President and Treasurer of the women group). At the maximum of Rs.10 to 20 per month, every member provide their savings. Each group consists of 10 to 15 Neo-literates of PLC in a village. After a few months, the saved money was invested in productive activities at a small scale level. The main productive activities are: Preparation of cooking powders, Flouring of Rice and Wheat, cleaning powders, soap powders, Blue drops, Jam, Juice, Bathi, Chips etc.,

Before getting the financial assistance from the Government, the AMI also involved in the productive activities with non-profit basis. The women neo-literates are participating during their leisure period. Some groups got training for tailoring, typewriting through the District Arivoli Iyyakkam. The Performance of AMI in Madurai District, before getting the Government assistance is given in Table No. :1.

TABLE-1
Performance of Arivoli Mahalir Iyyakkam before getting Government Finance as on December, 1995.

S.No	Divisions	Number of women Groups	Average Amount of Capital Invested per Group	Activities involved
1.	Madurai Corporation	79	4060	Sambar-Powder, Phenyl, Soap powders.
2.	Madurai Division	76	3055	Wheat,Rice Flour, Sambar-powder, Phenyl

{*Cont.*}....

3. Uslampatti Division	55	2637	Liquid blue, cooking powders, soap powders Blue Metal.
4. Periyakulam Division	30	2984	Wire Basket, Phenyl,Ink.
Total	240	3281	

Source : Computed from the Office records of Arivoli Mahalir Iyyakkam, Madurai.
Note : All women groups are involved in small savings activity and the same savings was invested for the productive activities.

Table - 1 reveals that during the period of 8 months, the AMI in Madurai district had mobilised the capital resource, at an average, of Rs.3281 per women group and they were involved mainly in producing the cooking powders, wheat and Rice flours. Preparation of Phenyl, soap powders, bule liquid etc. The study found the following main features:

1. Before getting the DWCRA assistance, the production was in a small scale level and they earn a meagre profit.
2. With the limited finance, there was no continuous production and irregular employment opportunities.
3. The members of the group had equally distributed their produced commodities at the time of marketing problems.
4. The women neo-literates were involved only during the leisure period in production activities.

In order to rectify the above difficulties and problems, the AMI had approached the District Collector for the development of the Arivoli women groups in Madurai District.

DWCRA

A mid term review of the implementation of Integrated Rural Development Programme (IRDP) revealed that flow of assistance to women members of target groups households or even women headed households had been very marginal. To subserve the overall objective of improving the quality of life of rural families living below the poverty line, a sharper focus on providing assistance to women as part of the IRDP strategy was considered essential. Development of Women and Children in rural Areas (DWCRA) was formulated as a sub scheme of the IRDP with in this frame work.

DWCRA seeks to provide income generating activities to women and also provides an organisational support in terms of a receiving system for the assisted women so that they can become effective receipients of goods and services available in that areas. Women's income is known to have positive correlation with the nutritional and educational status of the family and in the building up of a positive attitude towards the status of women. Hence, the necessity of ensuring more income earning avenues for women.

While the target group of DWCRA is the same as IRDP ie., families having an annual income of less than Rs.6,400/- (below poverty line). The methodology is through a group. The financial provisions under DWCRA are available only for the group. Individuals are financed on IRDP pattern from IRDP budget. The scheme envisages formation of a group of 15-20 women. The women are expected to come together for an activity of mutual interest to all. The entry point for the group may not be income generating activities but it must be an essential ingredient of the total gamut of activities in which the group is involved. The assistance available to a group is:-

a. Rs. 15,000 as one time grant contributed in equal measure by Government of India, state Government and UNICEF, which can be used as:
    i. evolving fund for purchase of raw materials and marketing;
    ii. honorarium to group organiser not exceeding Rs.50/- per month for a period of one year;
    iii. infrastructure support (seed money) for income generating activities; and
    iv. one time expenditure on child care facilities,
b. Traveling allowance at Rs.200/- for one year for the group organiser.

If the group is registered under the Registration of Societies Act, it can take loan from the bank as a group for economic activities. Individual women members will be entitled to subsidy as per IRDP norms and each member will be equally liable for repayment of the loan. In case the group is informal, it is not able to draw loan from the bank as a group and the composite loan may be disaggregated into individual loans and subsidies, with the group guaranteeing the total amount of loan.

Training of Rural Youth for Self Employment (TRYSEM) is expected to cater to fulfilling the skill requirements for beneficiaries of DWCRA also. The curricula, duration of training and rate of payment to trainers and trainees requiring the same should be in accordance with the norms of TRYSEM.

In Madurai District, the Arivoli Mahalir Iyyakkam registered under the Registration of Societies Act are eligible to get loan from the bank under DWCRA Assistance.

ARIVOLI MAHALIR IYYAKKAM AFTER DWCRA ASSISTANCE

As on Ist June 1996, the total members of AMI are 10,840 and number of women groups are 770 in all villages of Madurai District. The details of members enrolment in AMI is given in Table - 2. The table reveals that the 770 women groups were formed under AMI in Madurai District. Of the total women groups, a large number of groups (28.96 per cent) were formed in Madurai Division and lower number of groups (21.56 per cent) were formed in Usilampatti division.

TABLE2

Arivoli Women Groups as on Ist June, 1996.

S.No.	Divisions	Number of Groups	Total Number of Members
1.	Madurai Corporation	192 (24.94)	2812
2.	Madurai Division	223 (28.96)	3290
3.	Usilampatti	166 (24.56)	2298
4.	Periyakulam	189 (24.54)	2440
		770	10,840

Source: Computed from Office records of AMI, Madurai.

For the administrative convenience, the Madurai District was divided into 4 divisions under total literacy and post literacy campaign. The AMI got the DWCRA assistance in two stages. At the first stage, January 1996, 103 women groups got the assistance at the rate of Rs.15,000/- per group in Madurai District. During the period June 1996, another 113 women groups got the assistance under DWCRA at the rate of Rs.25,000 per group. A total of 226 women groups got the assistance of Rs.43.70 crores under DWCRA scheme.

The activities of AMI under DWCRA scheme are given in Table No.3. It is clear from the table that the 216 self help groups, in addition with their savings and by using DWCRA assistance, have involved in the rural enterprise development such as preparation of cooking powders (18.06 percent) rearing milch animals (12.5 percent), running fair price shops (12.5 percent), providing domestic credit/household credit needs (10.19 percent), production of ink, shampoo, cleaning powders, Jam, pickle, bakery etc., (9.72 percent) in Madurai District. The above said activities were predominantly done by the groups.

A lower percent of groups had involved in tailoring (8.79 percent) renting cooking vessels and ornaments for marriage purpose and running canteen in BDO Office, (6.48 percent), weaving (1.85 percent), blue liquid, phenyl production (9,72 percent) quarry and blue metal work (9.72 percent), wire basket and bags designing (4.17 percent), and preparation of wheat and Rice flour (6.48 percent), It is inferred that most of the women groups had concentrated mainly on fair price shops, rearing milch animals and domestic credit activities.

RURAL ENTERPRISE DEVELOPMENT BY AMI - FEW CASE STUDIES:

The performance and achievements of the Arivoli Mahalir Iyyakkam in Madurai District in employment and income generating activities through the rural enterprise development are discussed in this section. The research team had visited many villages (nearly 20 villages) and investigated the 30 women groups about the functioning of the women groups with the DWCRA assistance. The findings of the field visit are summarised below with a few case study analysis.

TABLE-3
Rural Enterprise Activities of AMI with DWCRA Assistance.

S.No.	Activities	Number of Women groups	Percentage
1.	Cooking Powders	39	18.06
2.	Tailoring, Typewriting	19	8.79
3.	Milch Animals	27	12.50
4.	Cooking vessels, Canteens	14	6.48
5.	Weaving	4	1.85
6.	Fair price Shops	27	12.50
7.	Blue Liquid, Phenyl	21	9.72
8.	Quarry and Blue Metal Work	6	2.78
9.	Wire Basket and Bags	9	4.17
10.	Ink, Shampoo, Cleaning Powder	14	6.48
11.	Wheat, Rice Flour	14	6.48
12.	Domestic Credit/Household Credit Needs	22	10.19
		216	100

Source : Office Records, AMI, Madurai.

Fair price shops

The AMI in Madurai District had involved in running the 27 fair price shops in various villages. In addition to the DWCRA assistance, the Madurai District Co-operative Bank had provided the loan assistance to the women groups for running the ration shops. Nearly 200 card holders got the benefits in each fair price shop of the women teams. The women groups are supplying the very essential commodities through the ration shops. The supplied commodities are rice, kerosene, sugar and wheat at reasonable rate with the correct weight measurement.

In Vachampatti, Keelavazhvu Panchayat Union of Madurai District, one AMI group under the president of Mrs.M. Thavamani is running the ration shop service to the public from September 1995 with the assistance of DWCRA and Madurai District Co-operative Bank. The experience gained from the fair price shops in Vachampatti are reviewed below:

i. The fair price shops run by the AMI charged a lower price for all esential commodities than the shops run by the CMS Marketing Society. Both the AMI and CMS Marketing Society purchased the commodities from the Pandian Super Market, Madurai. But they charged the different prices. These findings are presented in Table No.4.

TABLE -4

Rates Charged By The Ami And Cms Marketing Society In F P Shops In Vachampatti.

S.No.	Commodities	Rate charged By CMS Marketing Society	AMI	Quantity supplied per Month
1.	Rice -I Quality	4.00	3.75	20 Kgs.
2.	Sugar (1 Kg)	9.25	9.05	1/2 Kg.per unit
3.	Wheat (1 Kg)	4.75	4.50	3 to 5 Kgs.,
4.	Kerosene (1 lit)	3.25	3.00	3 litres

Source: Field visit at Vachampatti Village.

ii. The AMI Groups had charged the profit of 13 percent for rice, 14 percent for wheat and 70 paise per Kg., of sugar at the selling price, as per the Government norms. In addition to this profit, the used gunny bags are calculated as an additional income.

iii. The gross profit includes the transport cost and salary to one sales girl and one assistant. Two women got the employment regularly in each ration shops. One sales girl got the salary of Rs.250 per month and one assistant got Rs.150 per month.

Mrs. Thavamani, President of the AMI in Vachampatti village revealed some difficulties and suggestions for the successful functioning of Fair Price shops by the AMI group in all villages. They are:-

i. Lack of accommodation for shops - Now in Vachampatti, the ration shop is conducted by the AMI in the community hall of the village. It lacks storage facilities, lighting facilities, etc.,

ii. The AMI group are purchasing the commodities from the Pandian Super Market at Government rate. But the Pandian Super Market is supplying the underweight bags of sugar and rice to the maximum of 2 to 3 kgs per quintal.

These are the main problems faced by AMI Group in running the ration shops in Vachampati. The president is very happy to say that the beneficiaries of the ration shop are satisfied with the ration shop run by the AMI because, they are receiving the essential commodities at lower price and with the correct weight measurement. The problems could be solved by providing the buildings, supply of goods at correct weight and in the sufficient level to the ration shops.

Production of soap powder

A team consisting 15 members under the presidentship of Mrs.panchavarnam (30 years old) is producing soap powder in large quantities before and after getting DWCRA assistance, in Achampattu. In the initial stages, each member invest Rs.400/- for the production of soap powder (Surf Powder). During their leisure period, they are preparing the powders for two hours per day. The team got the training for the preparation of soap powders from the Arivoli Mahalir Iyyakam at the central level.

A Book "China China Ettu Eaduthu" published by Bharat Gyan Vigyan Samiti (BGVS) Resource Centre, Madurai is useful for the production of soap powder and all other products. The required raw materials for producing the soap powder are washing soda (1 Kg.,) R.P.Soda (3/4Kg.,) Sillary (250 ml.,) D. Blue (10gm), Dinopal (10 gm), Tri - sodium - phosphate (TSP) (30gm), STPP (20gm), and Scent (10 ml). By using these materials, the team produces 2 kg., of soap powder every time. At an average, the team has produced 20 Kg of soap powder per month before getting DWCRA assistance.

After getting the DWCRA assistance, the team continues the production of soap powder and also involved in providing the domestic credit needs in the Achampattu village of Madurai District.

The Group sells the soap powder at the rate of Rs 3.50 per 100 grams and earns the total sales revenue of Rs. 35 for 1 kg., production. The actual cost of production is only Rs.21 and earns a profit of Rs.14 per Kg., Mrs. Panchavarnam revealed some difficulties as follows:

i. Without publicity and advertisement, it is difficult to market the product in the open market, even though, the products of AMI group is sold in the market at lower price than the established company product, for example, 'SURF' - Rs.28 for 1/2 Kg., and the AMI group products - Rs.35 for 1 Kg.,

ii. The produced soap powders are equally distributed among the members for avoiding the difficulties in marketing and the group also losses the profits from the production.

iii. The group have to face the dangerous effects without using the hand gloves at the time of preparation.

If the AMI got the marketing facilities in the centre of the Madurai city by establishing a shop and make some advertisement of such products, the above said problems could be solved and the women entrepreneurs development in an unexpected level.

Production of Phenyl

The research team had visited the phenyl production centre at A.Vellalapatti, Mellur Block. The group consisting of 12 members is headed by S.Indira. They are producing the phenyl as per the suggestion of the book "Chine, China Etta Eduthu" and training by the AMI of Madurai District.

The requirements for producing the pheynl are: Pine oil (500 ml), soft soap (250 gm), Rosanam (125gm), Jasmine Scent (10ml), by using these materials, the group has produced 15 bottles of phenyl. The cost of production was Rs.4/- per bottle. But the phenyl was sold at the rate of Rs.9 per bottle.

In order to solve the marketing problem, the group approached the private clinics and Government Hospital in Mellur and sell the phenyl regularly to the hospitals. The Group earns a regular income through the production of phenyl. The group also sell the product at the lower rate than the market rate of the established products.

Canteen by women group at BDO office

The Arivoli Mahalir Iyyakkam in Madurai District is running the 7 canteens in panchayat Union Offices, namely, Usilampatti, Chellampatti, Sedappatti, T. Kallupatti, Thiruparankundram, Madurai

West and Vadipatti. The Canteen is functioned in the DWCRA Building in every Panchayat Union Office. The women group is paying a rent of Rs.150/- per month. The experiences gained from the Thirupparankundram canteen run by the women group are discussed in this section.

A women group consisting of 10 members under the presidentship of Mrs.Santha, Palaniammal (Secretary) and S. Padma (Treasurer) was formed on 30.10.1995. At the initial stage, the group involved in preparing the cooking powders and turmeric powders. Before getting the DWCRA assistance, the group earns Rs.100 per member from the production of cooking powder etc., After getting the DWCRA assistance, the team involved in running the DWCRA canteen at Thirupparankundram Panchayat Union office. The team got the DWCRA assistance of Rs. 15,000/- on January 26, 1996 and the canteen was started on the same date.

Of the total 10 members, 7 women are actually involved in the canteen work. Everyday, the canteen is functioning from 9 A.M. to 7 P.M., and the items supplied in the canteen are : Tea, Coffee, Milk, Vadai and the Variety rice, meals etc. The total sales, at an average, per day is Rs.800/- They earn the 25 to 30 percent of profit from the total sales. The seven women member working in the canteen got the salary of Rs.25 per day. They got the employment for 5 days a week except Saturday and Sunday. In the mean time, the excess of unsold items are also used by the members. The group is also supplying the food items for bulk orders like marriage and the ceremonies. During the period of 8 months period, the group repaying the DWCRA loan was Rs.2,250.

The only problem revealed by the women group (Mrs.Santha) is that the rent charged by the Panchayat Union Office for the Canteen building. The research team find the speciality of the group, at the time of field visit, that all women members equally shared their work in the canteen and they got the equal salary of Rs.25 per day per head.

Milk depot

In Achampatti Panchayat, a women team was formed under AMI in the year 1995 with 16 scheduled caste members including 14 neo-literates and 1 volunteer Instructor of Post Literacy campaign. The group started the savings of Rs.10/- per month. Before getting the DWCRA assistance, the members were involved in producing cooking powders, phenyl and blue drops. Most of the members are having one milch animals in their houses. The neglected scheduled caste people did not get the benefit of IRDP, so far, in this village. Only after forming the women group, the members get the DWCRA assistance through the AMI of Madurai District.

Mrs. Meenakshi is the Secretary for the group. She made some important observations about the running of milk depot with the assistance of Rs.15,000 under DWCRA scheme.

They are as follows:-

i. Of the total DWCRA assistance, Rs.10,000 was distributed to the women member having a milch animals, as advance, for the regular supply of milk to the women group.
ii. The remaining Rs.5,000 were used to purchase 3 milch animals for the women group and handed over to 3 women members for rearing.
iii. There are 3 women members involved in this activities as full time for account maintenance, procurement of milk and cleaning the vessels and supply of milk to the hotels in towns.
iv. The milk turnover per day is 38 litres in the morning and 21 litres in the evening.
v. The milk purchased at the rate of Rs.6 per litre from the members and sold to the hotels and to the public at the rate of Rs.8 per litre. But the actual market rate for the milk is Rs.9 per litre.
vi. After deducting the salary for the 3 women members (a total of Rs.2,000 per month), the remaining profit was utilised for repayment of loan. The women group, so far, repaid the amount of Rs.1,000/- to the Bank.

The women group pointed out some difficulties and problems in rearing milch animals under DWCRA scheme. They are,

i. There is no separate building for running the milk depot and for improving the enterprise.
ii. The financial assistance of Rs.15,000/- is not enough to purchase the High breed variety of Milch animals.
iii. The members have to purchase the fodder for their milch animals from the town on credit due to the financial problem.

These problems could be solved by providing separate buildings, enhancing the DWCRA assistance to Rs.30,000/- per group and setting up of a store for milch animal fodder by the women group of AMI of Madruai District.

The AMI has also developed such type of milch animals programme in Ayyappanayakkanpatti, Vadipatti Block and in Alanganllur Panchayat Union.

In conclusion, empowering women though the employment and income generating activities under Arivoli Mahalir Iyyakkam of Madurai District is successful in reducing the gender gap and development of women after getting education through the Mass Literacy campaign. Such type of voluntary organisations could be encouraged by the Government and the Public for the Women's Movement.

BIBLIOGRAPHY

BOOKS

Arrove and H.J. Graft (eds) *National Literacy Campaigns: Historical and cooperative Perspectives*, Plenum Press, New York, 1987.

Athreya, V.B, and Rani chumkath, *Literacy and Empowerment*, Saga Publication, New Delhi, 1996.

Anil Bordia, (ed) *Adult Education in India: A Book of Reading,* Nachiveta publication, Bombay, 1873.

Amil Bordia *Planning and Administration of National Literacy Programme : The Indian Experience,* International Institute for Educational Planning, Paris, UNESCO, 1985.

Bataille L.(ed), *A Turning Point for Literacy and Empowerment*, Sage Publications, New Delhi, 1996.

BGVS, *Total Literacy Campaign - A Guide Book*, Bharat Gyan Vigyan Samithi, New Delhi, 1989.

Bhat, S.S, *Growth and Development of Adult Education*, Cosmo publications, New Delhi, 1992.

Bhargave and P.C. Saxena, P.K. " Female work participation and Age at Marriage in an urban setting", (ed) K.Srinivasan, *Dynamic of Population and Family Welfare*, Himalaya Publishing House, Bombay, 1985.P.P.264-71.

Gandotra, M.M. "*Fertility, Mortality and Contraceptive Prevalence in the Dungs.*" Population Research Centre, Faculty of Science, Boroada, 1987.

Bhola, H.S. *Campaigning for literacy*, UNESCO, Paris, 1980.

Chandrasekar, S. "*Infant Mortality, Population Growth and Family Planning in India*", George Allan and Unwin Ltd., London, 1972.

Henry E. Garrett and R.S. Wordsworth, *Statistics in Psychology and Education*, Vakils, Fobber and Simons Pvt. Ltd., Bombay, 1971.

ISST, *Adult Education for Women - Eight case Studies*, Institute of Social Studies Trust, Ministry of Education and culture, 1984.

Jayagopal R., *Adult Learning*, Department of Adult and continuing Education, University of Madras, Madras, 1985.

Kapoor, M., *Women and Family Life Education in India*, Print well, Jaipur,. 1986.

Krishna Raj, M. (ed) *Women's Studies in India,* Popular Prakashan, Bombay, 1986.

Mathur, R.S., *Literacy Digest*, Directorate of Adult Education, New Delhi, 1988.

Mishra L., *The Turning Point*, Government of India, Directorate of Adult Education, New Delhi, 1990.

Moonis Raya and H. Ramachandran, *Schooling and Rural Transformation,* Vikas Publishing House Private Ltd., Bombay, 1990.

National Literacy Mission, *Post Literacy in Tamil Nadu*, Directorate of Adult Education, New Delhi, 1995.

NIEPA, *Educational for All by 2000: Indian perspective*, National Institute of Educational planning and Administration, 1990.

Pai Pannandikar, V.A. Ajay K.Mehra, *"Peoples" Participation in Family Planning*", Uppal Publishing House, New Delhi, 1987.

Prem chand, *Statistical Data base of Literacy*, Vol.I and II National Institute of Adult Education, New Delhi, 1992.

Pradipto Ray Joseph Kilin,"*Health innovation and Family Planning*", National institute of Community Development, Hydrabad 1989.

Prem chand, *Literacy Digest,* Directorate of Adult Education, New Delhi, 1991.

Qureshi and Samiur Rahman, *"Impact of Population Education on Learners of Adult Literacy programmes in Delhi: AKAP study,"* State Resource Centre, Jamia Millia Islamia, New Delhi 1993.

Rajeswari, N.V. *"A Comparative study of laparascopic and Conventional Tubectomy Acceptors in Uttar Karnataka, Karnataka"*, Population Research Centre, ISS Institute of Economic Research, Dharward, 1987.

Rama Rao, G. "An investigation into the relationship between infant Mortality and fertility Among countries under Different Socio-economic contexts," (ed) K.Srinivasan, *Dynamic of Population and Family Welfare,* Himalaya Publishing House, Bombay, 1985 P.P.185-213.

Rao, V.K.R.V. *Education and Human Resource Development,* Allied publishers, New Delhi, 1966.

Saraf, S.N. *Literacy in a Non-Literacy Mission,* International Institute for Educational planning, Paris, 1980.

Shah S.Y. *A, Source Book on Adult Education,* Government of India, Directorate of Adult Education, New Delhi, 1989.

Shah, A.B, and Susheela Bhan (Eds) *Non-Formal Education and the NAEP,* Oxford University press, Bombay, 1980.

World Bank, *Education Sector policy paper,* Washington, 1980.

JOURNALS:

Adiseshiah, Malcom.S. "Some Adult Literacy Imperatives", *Literacy and Learning,* Vol.3, No.6, Government of India, Directorate of Adult Education, New Delhi, 1988.

Athreya, V.B: "To the people: A Model for the Mass", *Frontline,* September, 25, 1992.

Arun Ghosh, Annals of the Literacy programmes: A Scenrio from Rajasthan", *Economic and political weekly,* Vol.XXVI, No.:42, Sep.19, 1991.

Adhinarayana Reddy and Ramana Reddy, "Suggestions of Field Functionaries on TLC Chittoor district," *India Journal of Adult Education,* Vol.57, No:3, July - Sep. 1996.

Ambika Jain, 'Mobilisation of Women through Education Training camp", *Journal of Education and Social Change,* Vol.36, No.9, December, 1989.

Baskaran V., "Women's Education Key to National Development", *Social Welfare,* Vol.36. NO.9, 1984.

Chacko C.K., "Fertility and Contraceptive practices among religious Minorities", *Bulletin,* Gandhigram Institute of Rural health and Family Welfare, Ambathurai, Vol.XIII No.2,1978.

Dutta S.K., D.K. Ghosh, Status of Women in Total Literacy Campaign: A Study of Birlhum District in west Bengal, *Journal of Rural Development,* Vol.14, No:1, January-March, 1995, P.33.

Express News Service, "Burdwan Moving Towards Total Literacy", *Indian Express,* Madurai, May, 27, 1991.

Jegannadha Saranak and Krishna Reddy, "Literacy in East Godavari", *Literacy Mission,* Vol.XIX, No.6, March 1995.

Hans Raj Gugnani, "Literacy: The Role of Media" *Journal of India Education,* Vol.XXXIII, No.28, July,11,1994.

Hemalatha Prasad, C. Development of Women and Children in Rural Areas: Successful Case Studies, *Journal of Rural Development,* Vol.14 No:1, January-March, 1995, (.65.

Israney S.M, "Status of Women in the Academic World", Indian context, *University, News,* Vol.27, No.23, June, 5, 1989.

Jeya Indiresan, "Education for Women's Equality-Policy Perspectives Vs Performance", *University News,* Vol.XXXIII, No.45, November 6, 1995.

Kerinston K., "Youth as a Age of Life", *American Scholar,* Vol.39, 1970.

Mahadevan Pillai, K. and P.R. Dutta, "A Sociological Appraisal of Raising Age at Marriage, "*Bulletin,* Gandhigram Institute of Rural health and Family Planning, Ambathurai, Vol.VI,No.3,1972.

Mishra S.K, "Empowerment of women through Extension", *University News,* Vol.29, No.21, May, 27, 1991.

Mishra Sharma and V.V. Saiyeed, "Differential Traits of Illiterate participants and Non-participants in TLC - A Study of Mangalpur", *Indian Journal of Adult Education,* vol.55, No:3, July-September, 1994.

Narayanan Namboodiri, D. "Caste, Status and Fertility in a Rural Area of Tamil Nadu", *Bulletin*, Gandhigram Institute of Rural Health and Family Planning, Ambathurai, Vol.VIII,No.1, 1972.

Nitsa Rao, "Total Literacy Campaign: A Field Report," *Economic and Political Weekly*, Vol. No.8, 1993.

Pillai, J.K, "Empowering women in India: New Roles for Education", *University News*, Vol.28, No. 7, November, 19, 1990.

Ramachandra Sastry,K. "Determinants of contraception. A study of adopters and non-adopters", *Bulletin*, Gandhigram Institute of Rural Health and Family Planning, Ambathurai, Vol, XVIV, No2, 1984.

Rajakutty, S. and Pritha Sankar, A DWCRA Odyssey in North 24 paragons - A Learning Experience, *Journal of Rural Development*, Vol.13 , No:3 July - September, 1994, P.375.

Reddeppa Reddy, M.C. "Differential rates of Literacy in India", *Journal of Indian Education*, Vol.XVI, No.5, January, 1991.

Radha Devi, "Sterlisation-an in depth study of factors affecting differential preference of vasectomy and tubectomy; timing of adoption and preoperative apprehensions of eligible couples", *Bulletin*, Gandhigram. Institute of Rural Health and Family Welfare, Ambathurai Vol.14, No.1, 1979.

'Raba Majumbar, "Education as Investment: :Low Priority and Small Returns for Women," *University News*, Vol.29,No.28, July, 15, 1991.

Ramachadra Sastry.K, "Why do some couples have more children than they actually wanted", *Bulletin*, Gandhigram Institute of Rural Health and Family Planning, Ambathurai, Vol.17-18, 1993.

Raj, M.S., "Non-formal Educational Schemes in the Education and Empowerment of Women", *Guru Nanak Journal of Sociology* Vol.10, Nos, 1-2, April-October, 1989.

Sarma K.J., and B. Krishna Reddy, "Literacy in East Godavari", *Literacy Mission*, Vol, XIX, No.6, August 1995.

Sita Vanka, "Education For All - The Problem of Dropouts among women in Hydrabad District", *Indian Journal of Adult Education*, Vol.56, No.4, October-December, 1995.

Shankar Mukerjee, "Total Literacy will the Dream come True," *Distance Education*, year 6, No.4, 1995.

Sivasamy G. "Literacy as Social Action: The Sundargah Experience," *Literacy Mission*, Vol.XXVI, No:38, Sep.21, 1991.

Sadhana Saxana, "Myth of Total Literacy in Narasinghpur", *Economic and political Weekly*, vol.XXVII, No,45, November, 7, 1992.

Soundarapandian M. " Total Literacy Campaign and Dropouts in Primary schools", *India Journal of Adult Education*, Vol.56, No:4, Oct - Dec. 1995.

Soundarapandian M. " Socio-Economic Status of Volunteer Instructors and Dropouts Learners in Total Literacy Campaign", *India Journal of Adult Education* Vol.55, No.3, July-September, 1994.

Soundarapandian, M. "Education and Demographic Behavior", *Journal of Education and Social change*, Vol,VII, No.4 Vol.VIII, No.1, January-March, April - June, 1994.

Srivastava J.N, "*Correlates of Age at Marriage in India with special reference to literacy status*" Fanatical Report No.33, Population Research Centre, Lucknow University, Lucknow, 1986.

State Resource Centre, *Approaches to the Mass literacy*, Paper Presented in the Annual conference of the TNBCE and SRC held at Madras on 1-3, November, 1995.

Sudha Sundaraman, 'Literacy Campaign: Lessons for Women's Movement", *Economic and Political Weekly*, May 18, 1996.

Sumarta Banerjee, "Uses of Literacy-Total Literacy Campaign in Three West Bengal District, "*Economic and Political Weekly*, Vol.XXVII, No.8, February 29, 1992.

Rajendra Pal and Hemant Khandal, "Status of Women's Education-some Expected Changes", *University News* Vol.XXXII, No.36, September, 5, 1994.

Saroj Pandy," Women's Education and Development in Orissa: PM Analysis", *Social change*, Vol.22, No.4, December, 1992.

Tarlok Singh, "Eradicating Illiteracy Among Women in Rural Areas", *Distance Education*, Vol.6, No:4, May 1995.

Vina Mayumdar, "Education and Women Equality", *journal of Education and Social Change*, vol.1, No.3, October-December, 1987.

Venkatiah, Education for All by 2000 AD, *University News*, Vol.XXXVIII, No:18, May 1, 1995.

REPORTS:

Government of India, *Report of Mahila Samkhya Programme for Education for Women's Equality*, Ministry of Human Resource Development, New Delhi, 1988.

Government of India, *Literacy Digest*, Directorate of Adult Education, New Delhi, 1992.

Government of India, _*National Adult Education programme: An outline*, Ministry of Education and Social Welfare, New Delhi 1978.

Government of India, *A Report of National Literacy Mission*, Ministry of Human Resource Development, New Delhi, 1988.

Government of India, *Status Report of Literacy and Post Literacy Campaigns*, Directorate of Adult Education, Ministry of Human Resource Development, New Delhi. 1995.

Government of India, *Report of the Review Committee on National Adult Education Programme*, Ministry of Education and Culture, New Delhi, 1980.

Government of India, *Census of India*, 1991, Tamil Nadu District Census Hand Book - Kamarajar District. Part XIII-A, Series-20 Madras, 1992.

Government of India , Census of India, 1991, Series-I Paper I of 1991.

District Collector, *General statistics*, Collectorate of Kamarajar District, Virudhunagar, 1988.

Government of Tamil nadu, *Statistical Handbook*, Department of Statistics, Tamil Nadu Government publication, 1991.

IOB, *Credit Plan for Kamarajar District, 1992-93 and Annual Action Plan for 1992*, Indian overseas Bank, Regional Office, Madurai, 1992

NCCERT, *Fifth All India Educational Survey Report*, National Council for Educational Research and Training, New Delhi 1989.

Office Records of Kamarajar District Arivoli Iyyakkam, Virudhunagar, 1990-91 to 1993-94.

President of Arivoli Iyyakkam, "*Report of Kamarajar District Arivoli Iyyakkam*," virudhunagar, 1991.

World Bank, *World Development Report*, Washington, D.C,1992.

INDEX

Adult Education Programmes, 2
Age at marriage, 134-37, 147
Age group of illiterates, 79
AIDS Research and Development Abstracts, 60
Akshara Keralam, 21
Arivoli Mahalir Iyyakkam in Madurai Dist., 167-76
After DWCRA assistance, 168-69
Rural enterprise development by, 169-76
Asan, Kumaran, 20
Ayyankali, 20

Bharat Gyan Vigyan Samiti, 3, 24
Bhargava, PK, 120
Brazilian literacy movement, 18
Burdwan, 22, 31-32
Burma Socialist Programmes, 18

Canteen by Woman groups at BDO office, 173-74
Castrol, Fidel, 18
Central Institute of Research and Training in Cooperation, 60
Chacko, Ck, 120
Chandrsekar, 119
Chattampi Swamiji, 20
Child marriage Restraint Act of 1929, 134
China's literacy drive, 17
Cuban Mass literacy Campaign, 18

Dany, 121
Directorate of Adult Education, New Delhi, 103
District Industries centre, 161
District Rural Development Agency, 161
Drop-outs in total literacy campaign, 30-57
Characteristics of respondents, 35-42
Date Collection, 55-57
In Kamarajar district total literacy campaign, 42-55
Awareness of, 42-43
Dropouts learners in, 44-46
Expectations of learners, 43
Implementors opinion about, 53-54
Measures to reduce, 51
Reasons for dropout, 46-47
Suggestions to reduce rate of, 48, 54-55
TLC Centres, 43-44
Training for volunteer instructors, 49-50
Volunteers opinion about reasons for, 51-53
Limitations, 33
Methodology, 32-33
Objectives, 31
Review of literature, 31-32
DWCRA, 162, 166-68, 169, 176

Education for All
conference in Delhi, 4
conference in Jomtien, 4
Ernakulam dist.
Fully literate, 21
Fair price shops, 170-72
Family planning, 139-41, 147-51
knowledge about, 139-41
Family size, 151-52
Farmer's Functional Literacy Programme, 11, 20
Freeman, 121
Functional education, 12

Gandhi, Mahatma, 10, 80

Gandotra, MM, 121
Ganeswari, VV G, 164
German Adult Education Association, 20
Ghosh, Arun, 23
Girl's early marriage, 137-38
Gradhasala Sangham, 20
Illiteracy, 1
  Elimination of, 1
  Population of, 4
Indira, S., 173
Infant and child mortality, 15
Institute of Social Research and Management, 13
Integrated Rural Development Programme, 160, 166-68

Jawahar Rozgar Yojana, 160
KAP study, 122
Kamarajar dist, 26-28, 33, 35-55, 161
  Drop-outs in, 42-55
  Respondents, 35-42
    Age-wise classification of, 35-36
    Caste, 37-38
    Educational level, 39-41
    Household income, 41-42
    Marital status, 37
    Sex-wise distribution, 36
  TLC centres in, 43-44
Kamarajar dist. Arrival Iyakkam, 26, 33, 35, 161
Kerala Association for Non-Formal Education and Development, 20-21
Kerala Shastra Sahitya Parishad, 3, 20-21
Kivlin, 120
Kothari Commission, 12
Krupskaya Award, 20

Lenine, VL, 17
Lincoln, Abraham, 79
Literacy campaign and empowerment, 160-76
  Arrivoli Mahalir Iyyakkam in Madurai dist., 164, 168-69
  Design of study, 161-62
  DWCRA, 166-68
  Entrepreneurship, 161
  Investment per job, 160
  Policy level, 160
  In Madurai dist., 162-63
  Rural enterprise development by AMI, 169
Literacy movements in India, 9-14
  After independent, 11-14
  By non-official organisation, 10
  During British rule, 10
  Gandhi's, 10
  Literature published, 10
  National Schools and Colleges, 10
Literacy Status in India, 3-9
  India's, 4
  Non-literates, 7-9
  Primary school enrollment rates, 5
  Ratio of literates to population, 5-6
  Urban-rural group in, 7

Macaulay, 10
Madurai dist., 85, 162-66
  Arivoli Mahalir Iyyakkam in, 164-66
  Literacy campaign in, 162-63
Madurai dist. Arivoli Iyyakkam, 164-66
Mahadewanpillai, 120
Malai Malar, 96-97
Mallika, G. 164
Management Information system, 21
Mass Literacy Campaign in other Countries, 16-19
Mass literacy drive, 10
Mass Programme of Functional literacy, 13
Maternal and Child Care, 141-43
Maternal care and delivery, 154-57
Meenakshi, 175
Mehra, Ajay K, 119
Milk depot by Women team, 175-76
Minimum Needs Programme, 12

Namboodiri, Narayana, 119
Narayana Guru, 20
National Adult Education Programme, 12-13, 20, 49
National Adult Literacy Campaign of, USSR, 17
National Board of Adult Education, 12
National Family Health Survey, 143-45
National Literacy Mission, 2-3, 13-14, 22, 117
  objectives of, 30
National Literacy Mission Authority, 14
National Policy of Education, 12
  Programme of Action, 13

National Rural Employment Programme, 160
Navanitham, S., 164
Nellai kattabommar Dist., 122
Nicaragua, 17
Nizamabad, 23, 32
Notestein, 121
Nyerere, Julius K, 18
Pad Manabhan, Mannathu, 20
Pai Pannanlikar, VA, 119
Panchavarnam, 172
Phenyl production, 173
Planning Commission, 160
Pondicherry, 22
Population, 116
Population education to neo-literates, 116-59
  Family welfare and health practices, 145-57
    Age at marriage, 145-47
    Family planning practice, 147-51
    Family size, 151-52
    Impact and Child mortality, 152-54
    Maternal care and delivery, 154-57
  Findings of study, 157-59
  Knowledge and attitudes of respondents, 134-45, 157
    Age at marriage, 134-37
    Attitude towards sex preference, 143-45
    Girl's early marriages, 137-38
    Maternal and child care, 141-43
    Use of family planning, 139-41
  Limitation of study, 119
  Methodology, 117-19
  Objectives of study, 117
  Profile of study dist., 122-26
  Review of literature on, 119-22
  Socio economic profile of respondents, 127-34
    Age, 127-28
    Community and religion, 129-30
    Family and housing conditions, 132-34
    Income, 131-32
    Occupation, 131
Puduvai Arivli Iyyakkam, 22
Puspham, A, 164

Qureshi ZH, 122

Radha Devi, 121
Rahman, Samiur, 122
Rajan, 32
Rajasthan, 23
Rajeswari, 120
Ramachandra Sastry, 121-22
Rama Rao, 121
Ramnathapuram, 122
  Profile of, 123-24
Reading materials to neo-literates under post-literacy campaign, 79-115
  Age group of illiterates, 79
  Analysis of materials supplied to, 91-92, 112
    Venue of PL centres, 91-112
  Assessment on, 94-111
    Books, 102-111, 113-14
      Circulated in PLC, 113-14
    Monthly and weekly magazines, 98-102, 113
      Neo-literates expectations, 101-02, 113
    Newspaper, 94-96, 112
      New literates expectations on, 97-98
      Newliterates spinion, 96-97, 112
    Primiers, 102, 113
  Illiterates lack awareness and action, 80
  Literacy campaign in Madurai dist., 8-86
  Methods of data collection, 85
  Neo-literates participation, 92-94, 112
    Distribution system of reading materials, 93-94
    Need of materials supplied made PLC, 92-93, 112
  Recommendations, 114-15
  Research methodology, 84
  Socio economic profile of respondents, 86-91, 111
  State Reference Centre, 82-84
    Role in education, 82-83
    Strategies in preparing materials, 83-84
  Tools for data collections, 85
Raddy, 60
Rangarajan, 60
Rural Functional Literacy Projects, 13-14
Rural Landless Employment Guarantee Programme, 160

Sankar, R, 20
Saxena, Sadhna, 31
Sazena, PC, 120
Schools in Aruppukkottai Division, 62-64
Students strength in, 64
Seetharamu, 61
Sex preference, 143
Soap powder production, 172-73
Socio-economic profile of sample respondents, 86-91, 127-34
Age group, 87, 111, 127
Caste-wise distribution, 88, 111
Economic background, 88-89, 111
Occupation, 111, 131
Sex-wise distribution, 87, 111, 128-29
Socio-economic status of respondents, 64-66
Somali's literacy campaign, 18
Srivastava, 120
State Adult Education Programmes, 13-14
State Resource centre, 82, 117
Role in education, 82-83
Sundaragarh zilla Sakshratha Samiti, 23, 32
Sundararaman, 32

Tamil Nadu, 24-26
Tamil Nadu Board of Continuing Education, 26
Tamil Nadu Science Forum, 24, 26
Tamil Nadu State Resource Centre for Non-formal Education, 24, 26, 32

Tharakan, Michael, 31
Thavamani Devi, T, 164, 171
Tirunelveli Kattabomman dist., 125-26
Profile of, 125-26
Total literacy compaign, 1-29
Elimination of, 1-2
Experiences in India, 22-24
Features of, 15-16
In kamarajar dist., 26-29
In other countries, 16-19
In Tamil Nadu, 24-26
Kerala Model for, 19-21
Literacy movements in India, 9-14
Literacy status in India, 39
Mass Campaign approach, 14
Measures for implementation of, 28-29
Participatory approach, 15
Programme and schemes, 2
Voluntary approach, 15
Total literacy campaign in school enrolment and drop outs, 58-78
Data Collected from school head masters, 64-74
Details of sample schools, 67
Drop-outs from primary schools, 71-74
School enrolment and TLC, 67-69
Socio-economic status of respondents, 66
Design of study, 61-62
Findings on, 76-78
Objectives of study, 59
Results and discussion, 62-64
Review of literature, 60-61
Statement of the problem, 58-59
Teachers and students participation, 75-76
Total literacy campaign Model, 3
Training of Rural Youth for Self Employment, 168

UNDP, 116
UNESCO, 2, 4, 12, 60
UNICEF, 167
UN World Population report, 116
Urban Adult Education Scheme, 12
Usha Devi, 61

Vietnamese Mass Literacy Campaign, 17
Vijayalakshmi, N., 164
Vijayalakshmi, S., 164
Vivekananda, 80

World Bank Study, 1
Writers Cooperative Society, 20